25.16

D0979570

Secrets for Secondary School Teachers

Second Edition

Second Edition

Secrets for Secondary School Teachers

How to Succeed in Your First Year

Ellen Kottler
Jeffrey A. Kottler
Cary J. Kottler

CORWIN PRESS, INC.
A Sage Publications Company
Thousand Oaks, California

For information:

Corwin Press, Inc.
A Sage Publications Company
2455 Teller Road
Thousand Oaks, California 91320
www.corwinpress.com

Sage Publications Ltd.
6 Bonhill Street
London EC2A 4PU
United Kingdom

Sage Publications India Pvt. Ltd.
B-42, Panchsheel Enclave
Post Box 4109
New Delhi 110 017 India

Printed in the United States of America

Library of Congress Cataloging-in-Publication Data

Kottler, Ellen.
Secrets for secondary school teachers : how to succeed in your first year / Ellen Kottler, Jeffrey A. Kottler, Cary J. Kottler.—2nd ed.
    p. cm.
Includes bibliographical references and index.
ISBN 0-7619-3984-9 (Cloth)—ISBN 0-7619-3985-7 (Paper)
    1. First year teachers. 2. High school teachers. 3. Teacher orientation.
I. Kottler, Jeffrey A. II. Kottler, Cary J. III. Title.
LB2844.1.N4K67 2004
373.11—dc22   2003015358

This book is printed on acid-free paper.

04   05   06   07   10   9   8   7   6   5   4   3   2   1

Acquisitions editor:	Rachel Livsey
Editorial assistant:	Phyllis Cappello
Production editor:	Sanford Robinson
Copy editor:	Teresa Herlinger
Typesetter:	C&M Digitals (P) Ltd.
Proofreader:	Doris Hus
Cover designer:	Michael Dubowe
Indexer:	Teri Greenberg

Contents

Preface

Excitement. Curiosity. Apprehension. No, make that *terror*! These are just a few of the reactions that new teachers have as they anticipate their first year in the classroom.

The book work is done. The closely supervised field experiences and student teaching are over. No more taking tests or writing papers—now you are the one who gets to grade them!

You now have the freedom to organize your own life, away from the confines of the university. You will develop the lesson plans and implement them. Finally, you will start earning money doing something you hope you will truly love. You will be responsible for molding impressionable minds in positive directions. It will be so great, you think, creating the kind of classroom that you always wanted as a student—a place where real learning takes place, where kids have fun, where there is order and support, where differences are honored, and yet everyone works together as a team.

Certainly, you have seen enough from your classroom observations and field experiences to know that there is tremendous diversity in the ways that teachers organize their classrooms and their lives. You have seen chaos in action—teachers who are jokes in their schools, who earn little respect from their colleagues and even less from their students. You have observed other teachers throughout your life who are truly masters at their craft, absolutely brilliant in their abilities to win friends and influence people. A few of these individuals may even be responsible for your own decision to be a teacher.

Now you stand poised, ready to begin your own career as an educator. You don't want to be one of those teachers who is eaten alive, who burns out after a few years—or even worse, who keeps teaching year after year, long after the point where he or she cares any longer about children and their learning. Neither do you want to be the kind of teacher who is average, who puts in the years, accumulates time in the retirement system, processes children like an assembly line, doing an adequate but undistinguished job. No, you want to be a *great* teacher.

Your dream can very well become a reality . . . if you make some sound decisions from the beginning. This means applying what you learned in your teacher education program in such a way that it is consistent with the realities of your particular school. It means catching on rather quickly to the innumerable traps and challenges you will face during your first year as a teacher. It means recruiting the right mentors who can support you along the way.

This book is intended to serve as one of your mentors, a handbook that you can consult periodically to prepare yourself for any of the usual challenges you are likely to face. It has been written by a teacher-administrator, a teacher-counselor-educator, and a student, specifically to reflect the realities of what most likely leads to success for beginning teachers.

We have brought together the most practical elements from your course work, from the education literature, and from the advice of master teachers to provide you with guidance during your first professional teaching position. The book includes tips and secrets that experienced teachers have developed to simplify, organize, and reduce the stress associated with the first year on the job. Many of the tips are illustrated with vignettes that show how they can be applied in action.

A series of brief, focused chapters addresses a number of topics that are absolutely critical for teachers. Beginning with the basics of orienting yourself to your school and classroom, we then provide specific and practical advice for not only surviving but flourishing during your first year of teaching. These issues include such things as getting to know students, parents, and community; captivating and holding student attention; organizing your room and learning your way around the school; developing lesson plans and assessments, dealing with sources of stress, such as being evaluated and dealing with difficult students; figuring out the culture of the school so you can make a place for yourself; and preparing yourself for all the things you needed to learn in school but somehow missed along the way. We cover pragmatic realities related to difficult students and colleagues, handling paperwork, networking with others for support, preparing for a substitute, dealing with disappointments and unrealistic expectations, as well as maintaining your enthusiasm and planning for your own future.

This edition features a new chapter, Developing Plans for Instruction and Assessment. It begins with a look at long-term planning and unit planning and then focuses on daily lesson planning. A suggested lesson plan format is presented and described. Attention is given to working with English-language learners, special needs populations, as well as literacy strategies for struggling readers. Next, formative and summative assessments are discussed along with traditional and alternative assessments. An "A to Z" list of assessments is provided. Both holistic and analytic scoring rubrics are presented. Finally, norm-referenced and criterion-referenced standardized testing is addressed.

Other additions are incorporated throughout the book. Chapter 1, Learning Your Way Around the School, now looks at the department chair and fellow department members as resources, as well as the role of induction programs. Chapter 2, Organizing Your Room, includes suggestions for traveling teachers regarding materials and supplies. Chapter 3 is expanded to address multiple intelligences, learning styles, gifted and talented students, sexual orientation, and diverse abilities in the classroom. Chapter 7, Managing Time and Paperwork, has more tips for organizing work space and looks at time management. Chapter 11, Communicating with Parents, emphasizes the importance of involving parents in their children's education, with a description of the National PTA Standards. Chapter 12, Engaging Difficult Students, identifies suggestions for engaging students with attention deficits, ADHD, and looks at prevention of discipline problems as well as mild and major intervention strategies for classroom management. Chapter 16 in this edition, Taking Care of Yourself to Minimize Stress, is expanded and includes a new chart on sources of stress as a reference, as well as sections on finding support groups and assistance on the Internet. Finally, Planning Your Future, now Chapter 17, includes a lengthy section on the National Board for the Professional Teaching Standards and a list of general education and specific professional organizations as resources. Additional technology suggestions are interwoven throughout the chapters.

Implicit in all of these topics is much of what you need as a beginning teacher, not only to succeed in your new profession, but also to flourish. As you are probably already aware, a significant number of new teachers, even those with tremendous passion, commitment, and enthusiasm, still struggle mightily in their first year of practice. Half of new teachers leave the classroom altogether within their first five years, so dispirited and frustrated with the realities for which they were unprepared.

This book is written for new teachers, as well as those who are in the midst of their education and training. Although the suggestions and structures we offer are based in research and practice, this manual is intended to be practical above all else. It provides you with all the little (and not so little) things that will help you to do your job in such a way that you make your classrooms fun, interesting, and challenging—not only for your students but for yourself. Because if you are not having fun working as a teacher, you're probably not doing it right!

The contributions of the following reviewers are gratefully acknowledged:

Barbara Slater Stern, Ed.D.
Associate Professor
James Madison University
Harrisonburg, VA

Dr. Judy Butler
University of West Georgia
Carollton, GA

About
the Authors

Ellen Kottler received her bachelor's degree from the University of Michigan, her master's degree from Eastern Michigan University, and her Ed.S. from the University of Nevada, Las Vegas. She has been a secondary teacher for over 30 years, in public, private, and alternative schools at the secondary level, teaching a range of courses in social studies, humanities, and foreign language. Formerly an administrative specialist for the Department of Curriculum and Professional Development in the Clark County School District (Las Vegas, Nevada), she is currently a Lecturer in Secondary Education at California State University, Fullerton, and a grantwriter for the Anaheim Union High School District, Anaheim, California. She is the coauthor of *Children With Limited English: Teaching Strategies for the Regular Classroom* (2002) and *Counseling Skills for Teachers* (2000).

Jeffrey A. Kottler is Professor and Chair of the Counseling Program at California State University, Fullerton. He has worked as a teacher, counselor, and therapist in preschool, middle school, mental health center, crisis center, university, community college, and private practice settings. He has served as a Fulbright Scholar and Senior Lecturer in Peru (1980) and Iceland (2000), and has worked as a Visiting Professor in New Zealand, Australia, Hong Kong, Singapore, and Nepal. He is the author or coauthor of over 50 books in education and psychology, including *Introduction to*

Therapeutic Counseling (1992), *Nuts and Bolts of Helping* (2000), *Learning Group Leadership* (2001), *Theories in Counseling and Therapy* (2001), *Travel That Can Change Your Life* (1997), *Making Changes Last* (2001), *Bad Therapy* (2002), and *The Mummy at the Dining Room Table* (2003).

Cary J. Kottler has attended public school in the United States and New Zealand. He is currently a student at Rice University in Houston, Texas, where he is majoring in political science and is captain of the rugby team.

1

Learning Your Way Around the School

"Visitors please report to the Principal's Office," reads the sign at the entrance to the school. Indeed, you are a visitor that first year, with all the appropriate levels of confusion and disorientation that are typical for an intrepid explorer who is operating in unknown territory without a map.

As many times as you may have visited a school previously, during field placements or perhaps even as a parent or relative of a student, you are always struck by how big the place seems. Everyone seems to know just where they are going, always in a hurry, making contact with as many people as they can, rushing to the next class before the bell rings. The place is a maze of offices, rooms, hallways, labs, each connected by a layout that probably once made sense to someone in charge of designing things. To the newcomer, however, whether an entering student or first-year teacher, the school seems hopelessly inhospitable.

ORIENT YOURSELF

Your first job is to learn your way around. We don't mean just memorizing the quickest route from the entrance to your assigned classroom; rather, we mean orienting yourself completely to every nook and cranny in the building. After you've gotten the official tour from the principal and department head, found out where to park and to what room(s) you are assigned, make it a priority to get "unofficial" guided tours from an experienced teacher, a secretary, a student, and a custodian (especially the custodian!). This is the place you will be spending most of your life during the coming years, so you will want to orient yourself as quickly and comprehensively as you can.

"I remember one new teacher," a colleague of ours recalls. "She never left her classroom during the day except to go to the bathroom down the hall. At first, we thought she was just snooty or unsociable. Only later did we learn she was so afraid of getting lost that she thought it best to just remain in one spot as long as she could." As you have more interactions with the staff, you will learn your way around and become more comfortable venturing out into other parts of the building.

As you walk around, note how the activities of the building are organized. Do the freshmen and sophomores have classes in one area while the juniors and seniors meet in another? Or, are rooms for specific subject areas grouped together, with science in one area and social studies in another? Where are the offices located? Are the counseling offices separated from the administrative offices? Where is the health office? How far away are the gymnasiums and athletic fields? And of course, most important of all, where do folks eat lunch and hang out?

Later on you will have time to notice where people habitually congregate. We are creatures of habit and take comfort in familiar spaces. Those who come early and those who stay late (students and faculty) tend to gather in the same locations. The same is true with respect to all the other factors that draw people together—their common interests, their age groups, their areas of expertise, their mutual attractions, and their coalitions.

You may be curious about how student lockers are organized—in most high schools, for example, students may be assigned lockers according to class level. You will also want to study where various student groups hang out—whether that is in front of the school, a quad area, or a specific hallway (and eventually you will learn the "secret" places as well). So, if you need to find a senior before school starts, you'll want to go to the "senior wing" of the building or the place where seniors typically gather as they wait for the first bell to ring. The office staff will have favorite areas as well, from lounges to department offices. You can be sure that most people, regardless of their jobs, personalities, or interests, develop consistent patterns over time.

MAKE FRIENDS WITH THE SCHOOL SECRETARIES

Most people think that the principal is the key person to know in the school. Well, she or he is certainly the designated authority figure and is ultimately responsible for what happens in the school. But the people who control access to the administration, the ones who are connected to all facets of the school's operation, those who know the most efficient ways to get things done, as well as the most important gossip, are the school secretaries.

In learning your way around the school, the school secretary will likely be your first point of contact. She or he will help you get settled, help you get keys and supplies, introduce you to other people, and guide you through the appropriate paperwork. Even if the principal does this him- or herself, you would be well-advised to spend some time getting to know the secretaries as soon as you're able. Ultimately, they can be your strongest supporters or biggest obstacles throughout your career. They control access to everyone and everything.

You will probably have a few thousand questions to address with your assigned school guide. Rather than overwhelming the person with the sheer number of inquiries, select the most critical ones, and save the rest to ask others later.

Here is a sampling of the most critical questions that one teacher asked her assigned mentor during the first few minutes of the first day:

- "Where's the bathroom?"
- "What textbook will I be using?"
- "What's my schedule?"
- "When's lunch?"
- "Does that metal detector really work?"

It is a good idea to avoid bombarding one person with all your questions and instead spread them around; that way you have an excuse to meet more people. Also, consider the timing of your questions. While most people are only too happy to help, be respectful of when and how often you approach them. Office staff, in particular, are often swamped at the beginning of each semester.

RULES AND REGULATIONS

The principal or secretary is likely to give you a map of the school, as well as the official *Teacher's Handbook* that tells you about the policies, rules, and professional responsibilities of your job. In it you will find the district and school mission statements; organizational charts; duties for teachers; guidelines for teaching about controversial issues; selection of supplementary materials; use of technology; child abuse reporting procedures; and policies related to grading and attendance, student discipline and safe schools, and other issues. Usually you will have an opportunity to go through the handbook during one of the new-teacher orientation sessions. Read the manual carefully when you get the chance, as it will include much useful information.

The handbook may contain the publicly espoused values, but does not necessarily describe how the school operates. To find out the "underground" version of the school culture, you will need to be aware of the interactions of quite a number of students and staff over time. This is how you will find out what is really expected of you.

You will want to discover answers to the following key questions:

- Who has power and control in the school?
- Who and what influences the principal the most?
- How do decisions get made?
- What are the major conflicts that erupt most consistently?
- What coalitions have formed among staff members, and on what basis do these groups maintain their membership?

These are just a few questions to consider. More will be suggested later.

Meeting Your Department

Most secondary schools are organized by department. If you are the single teacher in an area such as music, you may be grouped with other disciplines. If you haven't met the department chair, it will be important for you to do so as soon as possible. While the authority of department chairs varies from place to place, they all tend to serve as liaison between the administration and the department staff. In some districts, the chairs are responsible for scheduling and budgets; in other districts, this remains the domain of the administration. Your department head most likely will provide you with teacher resource materials and curriculum guides and inform you how to obtain texts for your students, supplementary materials, and supplies for the classroom. Some schools will have the department chair serve as mentors to new teachers; others will not make a formal assignment.

In some districts, the faculty members in each department do all their planning together. They write lesson plans and develop unit and/or quarterly assessments as a group. They meet regularly to review objectives and discuss student progress. You will find much-needed support readily available if this is your situation. If not, you will need to find a mentor in your subject area, preferably someone who has taught your assigned classes before, and who is willing to share his or her expertise and resources with you. If such support is not available in your school, you will be able to network at district-level meetings and professional conferences.

Your Classroom

Once you have been escorted to your assigned classroom and left to your own devices, allow yourself sufficient time to revel in the feelings that you are experiencing. This classroom is *your* room: the place where you will be working your magic. There are bulletin boards to dress up, furniture to rearrange according to your liking, supplies to order and put away. Mostly, though, you just want to get a feel for the space. Begin to personalize it, make it yours, at least to the point where it starts to feel a little familiar.

Sometimes you will be assigned a room or rooms that other teachers use. In that case, you will need to negotiate space with the other teacher(s). Nevertheless, you will be responsible for that room when your classes are scheduled to meet there, and your students will associate that room with you! The next chapter will discuss organizing your room(s) in depth.

Custodians

Another important person to get to know is the custodian. In the afternoon or evening, your room will be serviced. While a thorough cleaning may take place once a week or less often, wastebaskets will be emptied and a general straightening of the room will likely take place daily. Custodians will appreciate your keeping the room neat and having students clean up the areas where they work. Custodians may also perform minor repairs, help with moving furniture, and take away large boxes after you unpack. They can also provide you with cleaning supplies—paper towels for unexpected spills and all-purpose cleaners for desk tops. Make sure you communicate clearly the status of your chalk- or whiteboards. Clearly marking "Do not erase" on sections you want to keep posted will avoid problems.

BUILDING ORIENTATION

Once you have gotten settled, there are a number of other important places that you will want to locate from your room. These include

- Principal's office
- Deans' office
- Counselors' office
- Attendance office
- Registrar's office
- Health office
- Custodians' office
- Teachers' lounge
- Library/Media Center
- Main gymnasium
- Cafeteria
- School banker
- Graphic arts and copy room
- Restroom facilities

SAFETY CONCERNS

As part of your school orientation, you will also need to familiarize yourself with safety procedures in the event of some emergency: fire for certain, and depending on your location, hurricanes, floods, tornadoes, earthquakes, or volcanic eruptions. (According to a posted sign in a New Zealand school, in the event of such an eruption, you should close all windows and doors.) Schools today also provide for shelter-in-place protection. Your school district may have a system that uses color codes for the following situations that we have seen: (1) evacuation to the athletic field, (2) securing the perimeter with activities continuing, (3) remaining in classrooms with doors locked, and (4) all clear. You may want to note pages in your school handbook with bookmarks or Post-its for quick reference.

Check your handbook for your responsibilities as a teacher. You will probably discover that your responsibility for the students in your care continues should an emergency extend beyond the school day. If you have an elderly parent or young children of your own for whom you care, you will want to have contingency plans in place for them.

In learning your way around the school, make sure to find out where the fire alarm nearest your room is located, where to direct students in the event of fire and fire drills, and where the designated shelters and supplies are for other disasters. Fire drills are usually a surprise, so be prepared. Most schools provide teachers with a small first-aid kit for minor emergencies in the classroom.

SCHOOL TRADITIONS

Every school has its own unique culture and customs, some of them established by the administration, such as dress codes, others emerging from student or staff input, such as school mascots and school colors. Homecoming celebrations, school dances, and other events often have many rituals associated with them. These traditions are as much a part of the school experience as anything to do with the physical building, and you would be well-advised to familiarize yourself with these customs.

I (Ellen) recall beginning a new job in a high school that had more than its share of school spirit. Typical of schools in small Southern towns, much of the conversation during my first day was about upcoming football games that the Razorbacks would be playing. I listened intently to the discussion, trying to pick out clues as to what was going on, but I was lost. I had no idea what a Razorback even was. People were aghast at my ignorance and then dutifully explained that it was a kind of hedgehog, a creature with which I had had no direct experience.

The reactions of my colleagues got my attention so that I knew I had to devote considerable time and focus not only to learning the history of the Razorbacks but to other school traditions. In similar fashion, you will want to research how your school got its name, prominent people who went to the school, and landmark incidents in its history.

LUNCH OPTIONS

Part of your initial orientation should include exploring options for lunch. There is tremendous diversity in how teachers choose to spend their break time. Some prefer solitude to relax or go for a walk. Some use the time to work out or exercise. Others catch up on grading exams while they nibble a sandwich. For beginning teachers, we are unequivocal in our advice: You *must* use this time constructively to make important contacts, network with other staff members, and integrate yourself into the school culture—as well as eat! Too often, teachers lose energy because they do not take time to nourish themselves and replenish their reserves during the day.

In your first weeks on the job, you will want to experiment with different lunch venues: the school cafeteria, the teachers' lounge, and if there is an open campus, join different groups as they go out for a quick meal. It is not the food that is the issue, but rather the opportunity to meet as many other staff members as you can. In most schools, this is where many important decisions are made. Because the subject is so important, we will discuss it in greater detail in a later chapter.

MEETING OTHERS

Learning your way around the school most often involves meeting other teachers and staff members. This is where you find out what has worked before and what has usually been unsuccessful, and it is the way to get many of your seemingly endless questions answered. It is also where you will find the support you need to deal with the inevitable challenges you will face.

When you talk to others, remind them of your name. Frequently, there are many new faces around (especially after the students report to school), so it is very helpful if you mention your name *and* what you teach to facilitate the "getting to know you" process.

One secret to help learn the names of the staff people is to get a copy of the previous year's yearbook and study it intently. Some hairstyles may have changed and some pictures will be outdated, but the annual can be an excellent reference. In fact, there is none better to help you get a handle on the official goings-on of the school, the performances of the athletic teams, the activities of the fine arts departments, and the school traditions that are maintained.

INDUCTION PROGRAMS

Many of you will also be participating in a voluntary or mandated formal induction program. In order to provide new teachers with needed support, many districts and some states have after-school or school-day release programs (or a combination of the two). These are intended to orient new teachers to their jobs and responsibilities, as well as provide professional development opportunities. These programs vary in length (from regular monthly meetings to quarterly meetings), style (subject area meetings to conference format), and content (such as subject area, classroom management, assessment, and/or strategies for diverse learners). Some programs focus more on identifying areas of weakness for teachers (with the help of an administrator or an assessment test) to strengthen. You may even receive some university credit for participation. Some induction programs establish a formal mentor for each new teacher, while others leave that up to individual school administrations.

One of the nice advantages of these programs is that they will also provide you with the opportunity to get together with other new teachers to share your experiences. You will be able to talk about your successes, as well as commiserate about your frustrations. Most of all, you will realize that you are not alone in what you are going through.

TAKE A BREATH

The first year of teaching is indeed one of the most exhilarating and challenging time periods in your career. These remarkable experiences will remain with you for the rest of your life. You will be tested in ways that you can't imagine. You will learn some things about the world and about the process of learning that will surprise you. Most of all, you will learn a lot about yourself, some of which may frighten you, whereas some will delight you.

There will be precious little time for contemplation or in-depth planning. Your time will be eaten up by meetings, extracurricular activities, grading, and just trying to stay ahead of the students. Many of the things you had hoped to do will be put aside, at least temporarily. That's okay. Your main job is just to learn your way around, to get to know your students, and experiment with styles and methods until you find things that work best for you.

Be patient with yourself. Your principal and other colleagues know well what kind of stress you are under. They know you are inexperienced and will look for progress. Those who are harsh critics (and there will be some) often act insensitively because they, too, are under stress and treat everyone that way; it probably isn't personal.

It takes time, but eventually you will learn your way around, rest assured. Remember well what you are going through; before you know it, you will be the expert showing someone else around.

2

Organizing
Your Room

O nce you can find your way around the school, the next
priority is to organize the personal space in which you
will be operating. You learned in education classes that the
classroom environment is critical in setting the tone for everything else that you do. You know from your own experiences
as a student that there exists quite a different atmosphere in
a room that is drab versus one that positively vibrates with
energy. You also know that different things happen in a room
that is organized with desks in neat rows versus those
arranged in a circle.

The culture of your school, what other teachers are doing
around you, the subjects you are teaching, and your personal
philosophy of learning, will each contribute to the goals you
have for organizing your classroom. As you begin to set up
your room, consider not only your needs but also those of
students.

---

*I (Cary) always appreciated when the classroom was
arranged in a different order than the traditional rows, one
after the other. If the class size is small enough, it would be*

great to be creative and change things up a bit every once in a while. My government teacher arranged the seats in a big circle and she sat in one of the seats just like the students. In a way, it put everyone on the same level and encouraged more discussion among the students.

Another teacher would sometimes stop class and have us break up into groups of four, moving four desks together in a square for each group. It really doesn't take long to move the desks around and breaks up the monotony of the normal class routine. Spontaneity is the key to grabbing the students' attention.

I (Jeffrey) once shared a classroom with another teacher who had a very different style than my own. The first thing I'd do each day was rearrange the room with all the desks in a big circle so that students could see and talk to one another. I wanted a more democratic structure than a traditional teacher-centered classroom, one that encouraged interaction. Because this was a class in social skills training, this particular physical environment was entirely appropriate.

My colleague, however, was teaching a content-oriented course in a far more traditional manner. He was threatened by the things I was doing in my class that directly contradicted many of the values he considered most important: discipline, control, and authority. He believed learning took place through his lectures, whereas I valued student interaction. Our room arrangements reflected these pedagogical styles.

Because I was a new teacher, and because my colleague had a lot of power in the school, he worked behind the scenes to make me comply with his standards. The principal approached me apologetically, saying that he had some complaints because I was leaving my room "in disarray" for the next class. Perhaps it would be better, he admonished me, if I just left the desks "the way they were supposed to be." I was appalled, of course, but I learned a valuable lesson about how our own actions as teachers impact, and sometimes even threaten, our colleagues. In the future, I shared my plans for seating arrangements with my principal and got him on "my side" in advance. I also asked my students to return the chairs to their traditional placement before leaving the room.

We mention this object lesson not to discourage you from taking risks, experimenting with alternative classroom structures, or expressing your unique style through your teaching—quite the contrary. We hope you do create a class-room environment that is stimulating enough to keep students' interest and encourages them to think for them-selves and challenge ideas. Just remember: Everything you do as a new teacher is being watched by others and evaluated according to their standards.

By establishing routines with the students, desks can quickly be arranged and rearranged during a class period. If you share a room with another teacher, you will need to com-municate and negotiate not only how desks are arranged, but how whiteboards/blackboards and bulletin boards are utilized, as well as how desk, bookshelf, and cabinet space is used.

INVENTORY RESOURCES

The first step in organizing your room is to check out the resources you have to work with. Spend a few minutes sitting in different parts of the room to observe what it feels like. Where is the flag located? Where is the intercom speaker? Imagine you are a student sitting there, daydreaming about something far more important than whatever is going on in the room at the time. Note what is within the visual field from each point in the room. Listen for the acoustics as well, to hear how sound travels, both for sounds within the classroom and potentially distracting noises outside.

Survey where the bulletin boards are located, as well as the chalkboards/whiteboards, pencil sharpeners, lights, elec-tric sockets, overhead projector, computer, or any other avail-able equipment. Remember, when you use any audiovisual aids, you will need access to electricity and ways to avoid glare so the screens are clearly visible. If you have a telephone line in your room, you will want to position a desk and chair near the phone jack. Also note what type of heating or air conditioning system is used. Will students be subjected to strong air blowing on them, depending on where they sit?

Next, look at the furniture and equipment that has been assigned to your room. Do you have bookshelves, tables, chairs, desks, file cabinet, wardrobe, a computer? Is there any audiovisual equipment in the room? What items do you feel are most important? Start making a list of what is missing. Keep in mind that the resources available in your school may not match with what you were once told in teacher training was mandatory for good learning to take place. Technical aids are certainly useful, but they may not be absolutely crucial for good learning to occur. For now, make a list of what you need, and hold onto it until you figure out the most politically expedient ways to lobby for what you want. And if, for example, you are lacking computer technology in the classroom, find out how to reserve time in computer labs and/or the library for student projects, or see if there is another teacher you can be paired with to share a computer or audiovisual equipment such as a TV/VCR.

Most schools have a media or audiovisual center where equipment is stored. Sometimes, equipment is kept in each department. Even if you don't have permanent equipment, you might be able to gain access to things on an as-needed basis. For example, most foreign-language teachers have a television monitor, a VCR, and a cassette recorder reserved for them, purchased with federal grant money. Can arrangements be made for you to keep equipment in your room on a regular basis? Some schools even have opaque projectors available for your use. In addition, many districts have media centers with wide varieties of instructional materials available for teachers to reserve and use. In some states, the resources are housed at regional rather than district levels.

Check to see what supplies, supplementary materials, and curriculum resources you will inherit or have access to. Again, sometimes these resources will be stored in a department chair's room or other office, other times in a media center, or both. Decide where you will keep these materials and how they will be distributed to your students.

FLOW AND MOVEMENT

Room arrangements are critical to maintain student safety as well as engagement with class activities. From what direction will the students enter the room? Will they have sufficient space to walk by desks or tables with their big book bags? You have probably already given consideration to how you want to arrange the room to fit your teaching style and course content. Will students be listening most of the time or working with partners? How much will cooperative group work be a part of your classes? Will students need resources or reference material as they interact with one another?

Where will you place your desk? What will be on it? Will you have more than one "teacher work center"? Is placing your desk near a telephone a factor in your decision? Will you have a computer on your desk? You will want to keep your personal things in an area that is not easily accessible to students, yet is visible to you at all times.

Specific seating arrangements are designed to accomplish different goals. As you walk around the school visiting other teachers, check out the ways they have arranged their rooms. Note the advantages and disadvantages of each. Some of the more common configurations include these:

- Traditional rows of desks to maximize the number of students in the room and maintain order
- Rows of desks facing each other across a center divide to encourage student-teacher interaction
- Horseshoe arrangement with desks facing the front for maximum eye contact with students

- Tables seating small groups of 4 to 6 students for cooperative learning
- Desks in one large circle to facilitate student interaction
- A "fishbowl" design, with an inner and outer circle of desks

Of course, a combination of arrangements may be possible, depending on the particular learning activity. In fact, one way to keep students engaged is to devise ways that move them around from one seating arrangement to another. Nevertheless, you will still wish to settle on a relatively stable arrangement to begin with, at least to facilitate taking attendance until you get to know the students.

One other consideration in space design is related to managing student behavior. Because issues related to classroom behavior and discipline will be among your greatest challenges, you will want to make sure to arrange things in such a way that allows you full view of everything going on in the room. That is why many teachers prefer to use an overhead projector so they can face the students rather than turn their backs and write on the front board. Also, you will want to consider potential problems that could emerge. For example, some students will find countless pieces of paper or Kleenex to throw away. Their pencil leads will always be breaking. If you don't want students to cross your line of vision during your instruction, place the objects they need access to, such as boxes of tissue, paper, pencil sharpeners, and wastebaskets, at strategic points around, or on either side of, the room.

The larger your classes, the less flexibility you will have. Often new teachers have no choice in whether there will be desks or tables in their rooms. There is no sense whining and complaining about what you don't have in the way of resources, equipment, and furniture; for now, make the best of what you do have. Improvise as much as you can. Visit other classrooms for ideas. Begin a list of what you'd like to obtain, and keep your eyes and ears open for opportunities to fill in what is missing.

BULLETIN BOARDS, WALL SPACE, AND THE CEILING

The impression the room gives as students enter will set the tone for the class. Consider all the display space in the form of bulletin boards and blank walls. Because you can figure that at any given moment in time, more that half your students are in the midst of fantasy or otherwise occupied with thoughts about their families, friends, love lives, or lack thereof, it is important that you design displays in ways that are visually stimulating but not distracting.

With me (Cary) or most of my friends, we could care less about stuff like bulletin boards. I can't figure out what teachers think is so important about them. Who cares?

But my math teacher did something that was kinda cool. He put, on one of the side boards, a sheet of paper with the year, 1997, lettered on top. Then he had numbers going down the side from 1 to 100. Whenever you were bored or in the mood to do so, you could go up to the bulletin board and invent an equation using the numbers 1, 9, 9, and 7 whose answer would be a number from 1 to 100. For example, $1 + 9 + 9 + 7 = 26$; $1 + (9 \times 9) + 7 = 89$. The challenge was fun.

In spite of this skepticism, bulletin boards are useful for brightening up the room as well as helping you to emphasize key points of given lessons. They allow you to post general information about school activities. You will probably want to post the bell schedule and other school- or district-mandated announcements, such as the school mission statement and where to go for a fire drill. You may use some of the space to post current events related to your content area. Keep in mind that, if students face the front of the room, spaces in the back should be designed for different purposes than those to the sides or the front, such as motivational or decorative, because the students see them only as they enter or as directed.

You might want to hang pictures, photos, or posters to create a homey feel to the room. Students, and their parents, love to see their work displayed. In many schools, teachers are permitted to hang student projects from the ceiling. Some classrooms turn into museums by the end of the year, with student-created artifacts and projects!

It all depends on what mood and images you want to communicate to your students. In a history class, you would expect to see pictures of past achievements. In an English class, you might see rules to use for writing, or programs for plays, or pictures of famous authors. In a math class, you might see applications of formulas, geometric patterns, or famous mathematicians. But these are only traditional applications; you can be a lot more creative than that!

In deciding what to do with your bulletin boards, consider the following functions that are possible:

- Informative—Giving facts
- Rule giving—Guidelines to follow
- Demonstrative—Showing examples
- Motivational—Giving inspiration
- Stimulating—Posing a question or new idea
- Rewarding—Displaying student work
- Aesthetic—Reflecting interests and likes
- Reinforcing—Giving support
- Entertaining—Using humor

EQUIPMENT CHECKLIST

Before you put your plan into action and start moving heavy furniture around the room, first design a blueprint on a piece of paper, positioning each piece of furniture and equipment. Consult the following checklists for items you might wish to consider in your plan:

Permanent Features

___ Placement of door

___ Electric sockets

___ Bulletin boards

___ Light switch

___ Pencil sharpener(s)

___ Location of windows

___ Chalk- or dry-erase boards

___ Lighting

___ Telephone line

___ Stationary cabinets

___ Laboratory (science, home economics, art) equipment

Technology-related Equipment

___ Computer(s)

___ VCR

___ Audiotape player; CD Player/Record player

___ Television

___ Laser disc player

___ Overhead projector

___ Opaque projector

___ Screen

Furniture

___ Teacher's desk and chair

___ Stool

___ Podium

___ Wardrobe(s)

___ Student desks or tables

___ Wastebasket(s)

___ File cabinet(s)

___ Table(s)

___ Chairs

___ Bookshelves

SUPPLIES CHECKLIST

Once the furniture is arranged, you will next need to concentrate on supplies that will be useful in your work. First, take inventory of what is already available in your room. Then, make a list of items you will need, based on these suggestions:

- Lined paper
- Construction paper
- Scotch tape
- Book covers
- Stapler(s) and staples
- 3-hole punch
- Paper clips
- Pens
- Rulers
- Computer disks
- Hanging folders
- File folders
- Overhead markers
- Attendance book
- Scantrons (machine-scored answer sheets)
- Plain paper
- Masking tape
- File cards
- Post-it notes
- Pencils
- Scissors
- Videotapes
- Index cards
- Dry-erase markers or chalk
- Dictionaries
- Lesson plan book
- Multipurpose cleaner and paper towels
- Tissues
- Snacks to munch on (for you)

In addition to these general supplies, you will also need those related to your subject—chemicals for science teachers, balls for physical education, paint and clay for art, food for consumer and family sciences. Consult with your department head and other colleagues for suggestions in this area.

MAKEUP WORK

It is helpful to have a place in your room where students who have been absent can pick up their makeup work or a paper that was passed back when they were gone. Some methods that teachers have used successfully are these:

- A notebook binder where handouts—instructional as well as homework—can be found for each given day
- A file folder, posted on the wall or placed in a drawer in a hanging file or situated in a storage box
- A calendar posted with each assignment listed
- A list of assignments on a poster board
- An area of the chalkboard listing the day or week's objectives and assignments

FIRST-AID SUPPLIES

Easy access to first-aid supplies is important. Band-Aids are commonly requested. You will want to have the basic supplies readily available so as not to waste class time looking for them.

You will probably receive Band-Aids, a disinfectant, cotton swabs, sterile gauze pads, and gloves in a first-aid kit from the nurse's/health office. It is a good idea to include safety pins in the kit for torn clothing. For serious problems, immediately refer the student to the school nurse or health aide.

SUPPLIES FOR "TRAVELING" TEACHERS

Often new teachers receive schedules that require them to move from room to room for part or all of the day. Most teachers in this situation select one room as a home base and then use a cart to carry office supplies and the resources they need for each day. They prepare posters on large display paper, poster boards, or large Post-it notes that they can easily post when they arrive at the scheduled room. In each room, they identify bulletin board space and chalk or dry-erase board space to reserve for their classes. Their students are directed as to where to locate information pertinent to their specific class. In such mobile situations, it is important to keep the lines of communication open with the other teachers so that cooperation can be maximized.

Another secret is to color-code items for each class according to the room they will be used in. For example, use a red book cover on the text, red file folders, and a red notebook binder for course materials for the "red" room. It's also wise to carry "emergency" enrichment and/or review activities at all times. They will be useful in any of the following scenarios:

- you are called away from the class
- the students finish an activity more quickly than you anticipated with plenty of time before the end of the period
- you discover that students don't have the prior knowledge you expected in order to move to the next level activity

Even more important for "traveling teachers" is to begin and end classes promptly so that the room can be prepared for the next group. Establish routines for materials and supplies to be collected and desks rearranged at the end of the period, if necessary. Let students know where they can find you before and after school if they want to see you, rather than approach you with personal questions at the beginning or end of the class in the room you are trying to vacate. Since the between-class-periods time is limited, consider developing communication through other means (journaling, email, etc.).

OTHER CONSIDERATIONS

You may decide to bring some things from home to make the room more comfortable, such as a fan, a desk lamp, posters, magazines and books, and/or supplies. When I (Ellen) was teaching World History, I brought in a life-sized model of a knight's armor which I posted as a sentry by the door. The students enjoyed touching the metal, feeling how heavy the helmet was, and seeing how the visor moved. Some teachers bring in plants and comfortable chairs or sofas, space and district permitting. In most situations, these efforts will be greatly appreciated and not disturbed by your students.

In summary, how you arrange the space for learning is as critical as anything else you do as part of your teaching method and style. If the learning environment is uncomfortable, unattractive, distracting, or unduly plain and dull, you cannot maximize the possibilities for fun, organization, and focused concentration that will be necessary in the tasks that you plan.

Your classroom is your new home. In some cases, you will spend as much time there as the place where you live. Customize and decorate it in such a way that it becomes a comfortable base for your work and an inviting place for others to visit.

3

Knowing
Your Students

N ow that you've got your room out of the way, it's time
to concentrate on the students with whom you will
be working. Within a very short period of time, you will be
exposed to over a hundred students, each with individual
needs and unique names to memorize and pronounce
correctly. If you think that's overwhelming, just think about
foreign-language teachers who not only learn the real names
of each student but also their assigned Spanish or French or
German (or Russian or Japanese or Latin) names.

Learning the names of students quickly is only one of your
initial tasks; you will also want to accumulate some basic data
on each of your students.

COLLECTING INFORMATION

One straightforward way to collect information on your
students is to ask them to fill out index cards on the first
day of class, beginning with their names at the top. You can
also ask them to suggest ways to help you remember how to
pronounce their names correctly (such as with pictures or
phonetic spelling).

Not all students go by their given names. Many have preferred nicknames. Some are diminutives such as "Jimmy" or "Susie." Others are common, such as "Junior" or "Bud." One boy told me (Ellen) he wanted to be called "Boogie." I wasn't sure what to make of that, and I didn't want to embarrass myself. Because he wrote he was a football player, I went to see one of the coaches. I told him I had a student who wanted to be called "Boogie" and asked him what the story was. He assured me that it was okay; everyone called him Boogie.

On succeeding lines of the index card, there is room for all sorts of information. One line at a time can provide a place for the following:

- *Name and nickname.*
- *Address.*
- *Telephone number(s)* (sometimes students have their own telephone numbers).
- *Birthday.*
- *Age.*
- *Mother's or guardian's name, telephone numbers at home and work, and e-mail address, if available.*
- *Father's or guardian's name, telephone numbers at home and work, and e-mail address, if available.* You may also want to inquire as to what hours the parents or guardians work.
- *Language skills.* (Ask, "What is your first language?" then "What languages are spoken in the home?" "What languages do you read?") Here, you will learn if there is support in the home for English language (or foreign language) activities. Some students will not be able to get help with their homework in subjects such as English grammar if their parents or guardians do not speak English. This information will be useful in planning for communication with parents where translators or translations may be needed.
- *Interests and activities.* (Ask students: "Do you play an instrument?" "Do you play sports?" "What activities do you participate in before school? After school? Until

what time?") Here, you will learn what responsibilities your students have—who baby-sits, who cooks for the family when parents are at work. It's also important to know whether the student works or not and if so, how many hours per week.

I (Ellen) had one student who was always falling asleep in class, although he seemed like a very capable learner. At first, I thought it was a motivational problem, then that he was just being obstructive. Finally, I remembered to look at his card, and I discovered an obvious clue: He was working 40 hours a week in a restaurant. No wonder he couldn't stay awake in class!

Other information to ask for on the index card might include the following:

- *Goals.* What plans do you have for the future? What would you like to do when you graduate? Or, what do you hope to learn from this class? Some teachers like to ask what grade students would like to get as a way to find out something about their expectations for the course.
- *Something you would like me to know about you.* One way to provide students with an opportunity to give you information secretly is to ask, "Is there anything you would like me as a teacher to know about you?" This is particularly useful for gaining personal information. Students will write about things that they are not particularly comfortable telling you face to face or in front of other students. Problems are revealed: "I stutter." "I can't see from the back of the room." "I am really nervous about learning to drive." "My mom just had a new baby and the baby cries all night, so I don't get very much sleep."

You can personalize the questions to fit your subject area as well.

In a language class, you might be interested in knowing if the students have pets or how many brothers and sisters they have, because these can be topics for future discussion using basic vocabulary. In English, you might ask, "What is the last book you read or the best book you've read?" In a history class, you can ask, "What is the last movie or best movie that you've seen related to a historical period?" In any class, you might ask, "What would you like to review from last year?"

The cards quickly provide basic information about your students that will help you to get to know them. They offer an opportunity for your students to tell you some things about themselves in a private, non-threatening manner.

SAMPLE INFORMATION CARD

Cary Jay Kottler   Call me Cary.   Spanish name: Carlito
Born: Nov. 25, 1987   I'm 16.

We speak English at home, although my first language was
    Spanish when I lived in Peru when I was 2.
My mom works at the school district so I can't get in trouble.
    My dad works at the university.
Baseball is the most important thing to me. We've won
    5 State Championships in a row.
If I can't play baseball professionally, then I have no clue what
    I'm going to do.
Besides baseball, I guess I like music, movies, and girls. Once
    in a while, I will read a book.
I gotta tell you: I'm not crazy about Spanish. Hopefully, you will
    change that for me.

Although the information cards can contain a lot of useful information, remember to ask students to write legibly so you can read their answers.

One time, I (Ellen) misread a boy's first name and called a girl's name with his last name. Both of us were quite embarrassed. Sometimes, attendance lists are not provided until the second week of school, so your cards may be the only accurate information you have about who is in your class.

One nice thing about index cards is that they are easy to handle. In the beginning of the school year, the cards can be organized alphabetically, for taking attendance and recording grades. Later, they can be organized by calendar sequence so you can acknowledge birthdays. Being wished a "Happy Birthday" does much for a student's self-esteem.

The back of the cards can be used to keep records of parent contacts. Use the space to write the date, time, and notes about the nature of the conversation.

INTRODUCTIONS

It will take some time to get to know your students individually. A good rule of thumb is to model what you expect of others. If you want students to be open and forthcoming in the ways they present themselves, then you should be prepared to do so as well. Students admire teachers who are not only experts in their subject area but who are also compassionate, caring, accessible, and human. If you want students to be open and honest, then you will wish to demonstrate these values in your own behavior as much as possible.

You are about to create and maintain a community in your classroom, one that we hope will be based on mutual respect and trust, a place where it is safe to express ideas, to ask questions, to challenge thinking, to reflect on learning, and to personalize what is presented in meaningful ways. To encourage your students to show the requisite courage needed for contemplative learning and constructive risk taking, you must show them the way through your own behavior.

You may want to begin your classes with some sort of introductory exercise designed to help students learn one another's names, develop some cohesion and trust, and create a climate of critical inquiry. For example, you might ask students to give their names with adjectives that describe them whose first letters are the same as their first names. Some teachers like to ask students to do collages, fill in a "coat of arms," design a T-shirt, or answer a set of interview questions. The knowledge you gain will help you get to know your students. At the same time, you will be giving them the opportunity to get to know each other and build a sense of membership in the class.

Getting to know your students and helping them to feel comfortable with each other are the first steps toward a successful year.

Students' Cultures

We're sure you've heard how important it is to become aware of the ethnic and cultural backgrounds of the people in your classes. This includes not only race, but also subtler and less obvious elements such as religion, family traditions and dynamics that may be culturally determined, and the way gender roles are defined according to the student's ethnic and cultural background. For example, some students will not ask questions when they don't understand an idea or a direction because they have been taught not to bother adults. Questioning may not be valued in their families. Students may simply tell the teacher what he or she wants to hear—yes, they understand an assignment; yes, they can do a math problem—even when they in fact could use some help. Their cultural backgrounds may dictate that they are passive in the classroom rather than active participants.

One way to address this challenge is make an effort to involve each student in class proceedings. Try writing each student's name on a popsicle-type craft stick and keep the sticks in a can, pulling them out as you need "volunteers." Another idea is to instruct each student who speaks in class to select the person to talk next; however, the rule is that the student may pick only someone who has not yet participated. This ensures that students don't only call on their friends, and no one ends up being left out. Regardless of what method you use, it is indeed a challenge to achieve equitable participation in class so the same loud voices don't always dominate. Another secret is to pass out index cards (or have each student take out a piece of paper) and have them write down a question or response to a prompt for you to address in class. This way each person's contribution is included. You have the choice of including names or not. To see if students understand a concept, pose a question and have students write down their answers without identifying their names on the papers. This way you are not responsible for and don't have to take the time for giving individual feedback and recording grades, but you can see if students have mastered an objective.

Body language differs from group to group. Certain cultures teach that children should look down, averting their eyes as a sign of respect. Other cultures teach that a child should not look away but should look directly into the eyes of the person who is addressing him or her. To avoid problems of communication, the teacher must examine his or her culture and the culture of the students, and be aware of cultural differences when interpreting both verbal and nonverbal cues.

Your students may come from a variety of socioeconomic levels, as well. Those from families with high socioeconomic status (SES) tend to have stronger academic backgrounds, show higher school performance, and have access to more resources than those with lower SES. Those from lower SES backgrounds will need more support.

We (the two senior authors) happen to currently work in a school that the rest of the world will soon resemble. A third of our students are of Asian background, a third are from Latino origins, and a third are "other," meaning they are North American "whites," as well as European. The majority of students speak another language at home, and many are immigrants. What this means is that as teachers we can no longer hold onto one reference point of expectations. There is no "dominant" culture to rely upon as a norm. Needless to say, this makes for some very challenging situations that require flexible attitudes for adapting how we teach to an increasingly diverse population.

GENDER

Teachers need to provide equal opportunity for and interact equally with girls and boys. Title IX of the Education Amendments Act of 1972 guaranteed equal educational opportunity and, therefore, banned discrimination based on gender. In the early 90s, studies examined gender differences in the classroom and showed that boys received more attention from teachers than girls; are more likely to take advanced math and science and related classes; and continue in gifted and talented programs longer than girls. Studies also showed that girls received better grades from elementary through college, and though identified more often for gifted programs in elementary school, they did not continue in them. While later studies challenge these descriptions and indicate progress in this area, gender equity continues to be a focus area.

Teachers need to be aware of their own behavior, biases, and how they use classroom resources. When planning activities, involve girls and boys equally and use cooperative learning. You can do this by assigning seats that have boys and girls sitting next to one another, assigning group members rather than letting them choose their own, and calling on girls and boys rather than letting them call out answers because boys typically answer more frequently than girls. Take some time to develop a monitoring system (like putting names on popsicle sticks to pull out of a jar, as described above, or recording on a seating chart) to assure you call on all students equally. Find instructional materials that have male as well as female models and examples and that challenge stereotypes. Encourage and praise *all* students in mathematics, science, and reading, not just those who obviously excel.

SEXUAL ORIENTATION

Your class is likely to contain gay and lesbian students as well as heterosexual students. Teachers need to establish a safe environment where teasing and sexual harassment are not tolerated. Several court cases in recent years point to the need for school personnel to take a more active role in this area. Whereas states and local districts vary in their positions on this controversial issue, teachers must emphasize respect for all people and immediately confront harassment of any kind. Let students know that name-calling and derogatory comments are not acceptable behaviors.

DIVERSE ABILITIES

Students with special needs today are placed in the least restrictive environment possible. Therefore, you are likely to have students with varying abilities in your classroom. You may have students with visual impairments or blind students, hearing impairments or deaf students, speech or language impairments, physical impairments, learning disabilities, attention deficit disorders, mental retardation, or emotional disturbances. Even within each disability, there is a range of differences. Therefore, it is important to look at the specific profile of each student to learn his or her strengths and weaknesses. Each student with identified special needs should have an Individualized Education Plan (IEP). The special education teachers in your school will have suggestions for specific strategies to use with individual students. Contact the special education facilitator with any questions you might have. For those with severe disabilities, you may have an aide or a paraprofessional to help you daily in the classroom.

LEARNING STYLES

Students differ in how they receive and process information, but they will have consistent patterns of response. In order to promote student achievement, teachers must recognize their students' learning styles.

Sensory Modalities. You are probably aware that students receive information through their senses. Some learn best by seeing information; these are the visual learners who process the world primarily through observation. For them, graphic organizers, charts, tables, pictures, and videos are essential.

Others learn by hearing; these are the auditory learners. They prefer to hear new information. They would rather hear a story than read a book. For these students, learning is enhanced by audiotapes and videos. They may be particularly responsive to music.

Some students like to touch objects and manipulate them. These tactile-kinesthetic learners benefit from drawing, creating models, and acting out situations. Of course, a multisensory approach in the classroom will benefit all students.

Global/Analytic Style. This learning style refers to how people process information. The global learner uses the right hemisphere of the brain to focus on spatial and relational processing. This student goes from whole to parts, looking for patterns and determining relationships. The analytic learner uses the left hemisphere of the brain for linear processing. This student moves from the parts to the whole, looking for details on which to base an understanding. While students use both approaches, some tend to rely primarily on one style or the other. Teachers need to model both ways and provide student opportunities to practice both approaches.

Field-Independent/Field-Dependent. Students who are field-independent like to work alone. They enjoy competition and like individual recognition. Field-dependent students prefer to work with others. They like to collaborate and look to the teacher for direction. Again, teachers need to offer activities related to both styles—providing times when students can work individually without the teacher as well as times when they work with others under the teacher's supervision.

Impulsive/Reflective. Some students are quick to answer questions, make predictions, and guess solutions. These are the impulsive responders. Others are more reflective and take their time to reply. These students do not want to make a mistake and answer carefully to avoid errors. Teachers must provide ample wait time for students to formulate their responses and encourage other students to be patient. Reflectivity is a common mode of response in many Far Eastern cultures.

As you will see in the following table, by planning and implementing a variety of strategies, you will be well-equipped to address the learning styles of your students.

Learning Style Type	Sample Teaching Strategies
Audio	Verbal directions, direct instruction
Visual	Pictures, graphic organizers, videos
Tactile-Kinesthetic	Artifacts, models, acting out ideas
Global	Look for patterns and relationships
Analytic	Present details for analysis
Field-Dependent	Cooperative activities
Field-Independent	Self-directed projects
Impulsive	Ask for predictions
Reflective	Provide time to formulate responses

MULTIPLE INTELLIGENCES

Students also differ in their intellectual capabilities. Howard Gardner identifies eight categories in which students have strengths and weaknesses. They include: verbal-linguistic, naturalistic, interpersonal, spatial-visual, musical-rhythmic, intrapersonal, bodily-kinesthetic, and logical-mathematical. In planning lessons, you can use these categories as guidance in developing your presentations and planning corresponding student activities.

An easy way for a beginning teacher to address the multiple intelligences in the classroom is to assign students to do a project in the "spirit" of a given intelligence or have them

Intelligence	Teacher Support Suggestions
Verbal-Linguistic (ability to form thoughts and use language for expression)	Provide supplementary reading Hold discussion groups Have students do presentations
Naturalistic (ability to understand the natural world, flora and fauna, and negotiate in the environment)	Have students interact with plants and animals Explore the natural environment
Interpersonal (ability to communicate with others)	Have students work with a partner Involve students in cooperative learning
Spatial-Visual (ability to judge space in relation to people and/or other objects)	Bring in artifacts and pictures Do demonstrations Have students create models and pictures
Musical-Rhythmic (ability to create patterns of sound)	Play different types of music Use jingles, chants, and songs as a way of introducing and retaining information Have students put on musical presentations
Intrapersonal (ability to think about thinking, reflect, and self-assess)	Provide students with time to reflect and self-assess Have students create journals
Bodily-Kinesthetic (ability to move skillfully and manipulate objects)	Have students create and perform skits, role-plays, and simulations
Logical-Mathematical (ability to discern logical or numerical patterns)	Have students categorize information, find sequences, and cause-and-effect relationships Utilize inquiry methods and project-based learning

choose their own. They can work individually, with a partner, or in a small group. While it is not possible to plan for students to engage in all eight categories for each lesson, it is possible for you to give students the opportunity to explore each during the course of the year.

As time goes on, you will get to know your students and they will get to know each other through their participation in class activities. Through discussion, writing, and various demonstrations of performance, you will become more and more familiar with each student's personality and his or her needs and interests. You will also come into contact with other school professionals who will provide additional information, for example, through an Individualized Education Plan (IEP).

GIFTED AND TALENTED STUDENTS

Students with extraordinary intelligences and abilities will also be found in the regular classroom. These children learn quickly and can absorb more material at higher thinking levels if allowed to pursue interests independently. Often teachers will pre-test students to find their prior knowledge or skills and then allow gifted and talented students who show mastery to proceed at an accelerated rate or engage in alternative enrichment activities. Teachers can help these students by providing additional resources and allowing them to work on self-directed projects. Be sure to acknowledge their progress. Using flexible grouping will enable advanced students to work together to produce projects or presentations reflective of their abilities.

SPECIAL EVENTS

Alerting yourself to special events in the lives of students will help you communicate your sincere interest as well as encourage them in areas that are most important to them. If you know from the information you gathered that a child is involved in forensics, band or orchestra, cheerleading, track, or the school newspaper, you can keep an eye out for times when you can let him or her know that you are following his or her progress.

When I (Cary) was in junior high school, one of my teachers made a point of congratulating me for having my bar mitzvah. This made a big impression on me. It let me know she really cared about me.

My favorite teachers have always been those who showed me that they really cared about me. Like when I pitch in a baseball game, a teacher will let me know that she knew about it. Even if I don't really like the class much, I will still give that teacher a break in ways I never would with someone who just acted like I wasn't important to her at all.

When I have a problem or something, the teacher I'm going to talk to is going to be the one who seems to care.

Paying attention to rites of passage and giving appropriate recognition will help cement relationships. For freshmen and sophomores, those special moments include getting braces off their teeth and getting their driver's licenses (refer back to the index cards to watch for upcoming birthdays). Most teens get their licenses on the first try, but some do not and may be disappointed. Some are not permitted to get their licenses right away (for example, their parents may feel they do not have enough driving experience, or they may be punishing them for some prior behavior), and that can be a source of embarrassment. The first school dance or prom can be a time of great apprehension for boys and girls.

The big events for juniors are the college entrance exams. Results of test scores can be a confidence booster or a major letdown. For seniors, in the fall, early responses to college applications arrive. In the spring, the regular decisions on college applications come in. Responses to requests for financial aid will be forthcoming at this time. Also, invitations to the senior prom can be a source of apprehension and concern.

Watch the student and community newspapers for articles of recognition. Sports achievement is the obvious one to watch for, but check community organizations as well. For example, during the high school years, some boys complete their Eagle Scout training. Students enter all types of contests and competitions that they might not talk about in class: chess tournaments, writing contests, and so on.

Teachers often give examples of how their relationships with students changed in positive ways after they had observed students in after-school activities. One teacher related that after he watched a soccer practice, a student who had been somewhat belligerent was not a problem again in his class. So, whether it's the opening night of a play, or a choir practice, attending, if not participating in extracurricular activities is a good way to establish rapport. It takes time, but it is well worth the effort.

STUDENT RELATIONSHIPS

There is much to learn about your students, and they will reveal themselves in many different ways—through their participation in class discussions, their writing, their conversations with you, and their interactions with others you observe during class and through extracurricular activities. You will have the opportunity to learn about their families and their community. You will get to know some students more easily than others, so you will need to be patient and give yourself time.

As we will explore in greater detail in later chapters, the single most important thing you will do in your work is develop positive, constructive, supportive relationships with your students. This forms the foundation for everything else you do to promote learning and growth. It all begins with taking the first steps to learn your students' names and basic interests as soon as you possibly can.

4

Dressing
for Success

Teaching is a performance profession, not unlike that of acting on a stage. Our audiences study our costumes and decide, based on these appearances, whether we are convincing in our roles, or whether we are even worth listening to. Parents, colleagues, and staff, as well, form strong impressions of our skills and professional competence based on the ways we present ourselves.

In the beginning of the school year, it is particularly important to establish yourself as a person worthy of respect. You will want to create an image for the students of someone who is a responsible adult mentor, yet someone who is also "with it" in terms of being able to relate to contemporary fashion styles.

You would only have to go back into your own memories to recall teachers who wore strange shoes, or out-of-style clothing, or inappropriate outfits to realize just how important it is to dress for success. Your clothes tell a story about you, especially to impressionable youth whose identities are so tied up in their clothing.

First Impressions

First impressions convey strong messages. As you glance around the room and check out each of your students, note your own personal reactions to each of them. The girl with the three nose rings and studs through her tongue. The guy with the purple hair. The guy next to him wearing all black. The girl who looks like she just walked out of a fashion magazine. In each case, you automatically form a distinct impression and make some preliminary predictions about who you will like and who will be trouble.

Of course, many of these first impressions are inaccurate and misleading. Nevertheless, they do set up certain expectations that are often difficult to alter. For this reason, you will want to give considerable thought to the ways you present yourself to students and staff.

Clothing Considerations

It is important to dress comfortably, especially with regard to shoes, because you will be on your feet most of the day. Although high heels might be in fashion for women, a low-heeled shoe will be more practical. Although a flip-flop may be comfortable, it does not offer the same protection as a shoe or a sandal with leather straps across the front and a sling in the back.

Another consideration is the temperature of the room. If you are in a room that seems cold to you all day long, you may need additional layers. You may decide to keep a sweater in your room for when you get chilled. If you go inside and outside of buildings during the day, you will want to have a jacket or coat handy. In rainy climates, you will want to have a raincoat and/or umbrella handy.

Standards of dress continue to change, even in the business world, where more informal dress is becoming commonplace. You may notice experienced teachers around the school who appear perfectly at ease in their jeans and T-shirts. Someday soon, you, too, may reach a point where you can dress exactly how you prefer. As a beginning, probationary teacher, however, you would be smart to dress the part of the consummate professional: stylish, casual, and conservative rather than flashy. Dress codes vary from district to district and school to school. Look up the policies for your district. Is there a policy regarding pantyhose for women? Are teachers allowed to wear shorts? Check with your administration if you have questions.

Women will be comfortable wearing suits, dresses, skirts with sweaters, skirts and blouses, and dress pants with suit jackets, blouses, or sweaters. Men will feel comfortable wearing suits, slacks and sports coat, and dress pants with collared shirt or button-down shirt with sweaters if it is cold. Clothing should be clean and neat.

One of my (Ellen's) favorite stories is of a principal who walked into a secondary classroom and could not find the teacher she was seeking because the teacher looked like one of the students, wearing jeans and a T-shirt—an awkward moment for both principal and teacher. It's important for an administrator to be able to quickly locate the teacher in the classroom. Dressing more formally rather than informally will help avoid such situations.

Remember the age of your audience. Students develop crushes very easily on their teachers. I (Ellen) remember one boy who was cutting out paper dolls at the back of the room. I asked him what he was doing. He told me, with more explanation than I wanted to hear: "I'm cutting out paper dolls to dance all over your body." Hopefully, your students will concentrate on your words, not on your appearance. We suggest that you not wear clothing that is too tight or too revealing.

Certain disciplines will have alternate dress codes. For example, P.E. teachers usually wear shorts and collared shirts, often with the school emblem. But this type of dress may be restricted to the gyms and the fields. An interesting case in point is a social studies teacher and after-school coach who was informed he had to wear pants, rather than shorts, during the school day and would have to change after school to his alternate attire. This type of policy is, of course, up to the school or district to dictate. Teachers who have laboratory situations, such as biology, chemistry, art, and consumer and family sciences, may choose to wear lab coats to cover their street clothes while in their classrooms.

Spirit Days

Many schools have "spirit days" on which school colors are worn. Some schools have collared shirts or T-shirts with the school logo printed on them. Since people in general tend to wear T-shirts with jeans, figuring out what to wear on spirit days can be a problem. The challenge is to dress "casual" and show school spirit, but still appear "professional" and command respect.

On spirit days, female teachers might decide to wear the T-shirt with a jean skirt rather than jean pants. For either male or female teachers, black denim (if denim is allowed) or khaki-colored pants, rather than blue jeans, could also be considered. If you do decide to wear jeans, make sure that they are clean and in good condition. You never know when the yearbook staff will be around to take your picture!

Image

Whatever you do, you don't want your clothes to be distracting. Students will talk about what you are wearing rather than what you are saying. If you dress like an older brother or sister, you may be treated like one. If your dress is too formal, the students will comment on it. Clothing is a visual cue for middle school and high school students; it signals where they are and what purpose is at hand. It tells them what behavior is expected. Be aware that this is part of what your attire will convey.

It's important to look nice and take pride in how you look.

I (Cary) remember a teacher I had who constantly wore the same two dresses. It seemed like she just switched off every other day. This did not speak well of her personal hygiene. I'm not saying you need a different outfit for each day of the month, but it is good to make sure you avoid wearing the same thing all of the time.

Another teacher I had was extremely outrageous in her appearance, even distracting. She was weird. It was hard to listen to her because of the outfits she would wear. One day, she came to school with a red dot on her forehead like that of an Indian woman. We thought she was making fun of Indian people. We all wondered why she did that, but she never explained herself. Sometimes, she came to school with so much makeup on her face that she looked like a clown. Another time, she wore a red jacket with the Playboy bunny emblem on it. You can tell that we all spent a lot of time talking about stuff she was wearing.

I would advise teachers to definitely have your own style, but to make sure your appearance isn't going to detract from the task at hand. Because, believe me, it's a long year, and we students will be studying every part of you.

CLOTHING AS AN INSTRUCTIONAL TOOL

Clothing can also be used to emphasize points you wish to make in teaching. A Spanish teacher may wear a Cinco de Mayo shirt when he introduces Mexican holidays. A humanities or art teacher may like to wear a shirt with an impressionist painting on the front. A geometry teacher could wear a shirt with an Escher design. Even more inventive, an English or history teacher may dress up in period costume to attract student interest in a subject. A geography teacher may wear the dress of a particular culture being studied.

The clothing you wear becomes an extension of your whole classroom environment, as well as an expression of your personality. Give serious consideration to the kind of impression you wish to convey, and make thoughtful decisions about your wardrobe.

As we have mentioned, teaching could quite easily be included in a drama department as well as in education. Unless you are able to capture student interest, beguile your audience, entertain and delight them, pique their curiosity, and stimulate all of their senses, they are going to be paying far more attention to their friends and inner needs than anything you want to present them. Just as performers spend a lot of time thinking about their lines, their props, and their wardrobe, so too should you select clothes that reflect the kind of professional but accessible image you wish to communicate.

5

Beginning and Ending Your Class on the First Day

Your room is ready. You are sporting your single best outfit, the one that positively glows with confidence that you really know what you are doing (even though you are terrified). You've practiced your welcoming smile over and over, although if truth be told, you wonder how much of your apprehension and uncertainty shows.

You've written your name, room number, and bell schedule on the board (to avoid embarrassment for the student who has mistakenly entered the wrong room at the wrong time). You stand at the front of an empty room. The bell rings or chimes or buzzes or belches. You move to the doorway. In they come: students who check you out as they walk by, sizing you up and making their predictions about whether you are boring or fun, mean or nice, an easy mark or streetwise to their favorite games.

First Contact

No, this isn't first contact with aliens, but it might feel that way initially. This is the point where you begin, showing confidence and poise, pretending like you know what you're doing.

"Welcome, everyone!" You smile warmly. "I'm glad to be here, my first day in your school . . ."

The specifics of what you say are less important than the main objective of revealing yourself to the students as someone who does know what you're doing (most of the time), who is warm and caring, but also unwilling to tolerate disrespect. If you have a sense of humor, show it. But whatever you do, set the tone for what will follow throughout the year.

Make sure you have their attention when you speak. Project your voice so everyone can hear you. Remind students to check their schedules to make sure they are in the right place at the right time. State your name clearly so students will be able to pronounce it.

Give them some background on who you are, but rather than reciting your credentials, tell them a brief story about how you ended up where you are. If you have the technological support, use a PowerPoint presentation to capture students' attention. Let them know you *chose* to work at their school. You are promoting yourself in order to reduce your own anxiety level as much as those of the students, who are also wondering about what miseries you will subject them to.

Describe your vision of the class—what the content will be, how the time in class will be spent, what the students will accomplish. Be enthusiastic! Let them know you remember what it was like to be a student, that you know it's important that things be fun and exciting. You intend to accommodate them as best you can. Stress what they will be able to do at the end of the class that they can't do now! Let your optimism shine! Your interest and enthusiasm will be contagious.

Move to specifics. Tell them about the various activities they will engage in. If you have samples of the types of projects they might do, you could show them at this time. Let them see an example of the textbook, primary documents, and other resources they will use. Explain your role as a teacher, and your expectations of them as students.

Spend a minute or two on what supplies, if any, they will need—pen or pencil, paper, folder or binder, or any other subject-related equipment. Discuss any lab fees that might have to be paid and how to pay them (for example, go to the school banker). Realize the students may need a couple of days before they can get to the store to purchase what you have asked for or to get the money for the fees. Not all teachers give the school supplies list on the first day. Not all parents are able to take their children to the store the first night. Be patient. Be prepared in the meantime for students to come to class empty-handed for the first few days.

Also be prepared to be tested by someone early in your introduction, some student who is looking for attention, who likes to challenge authority, or perhaps someone who is just playful. Don't overreact. Just remain calm, poised, and firm. As we said before, show that you have a sense of humor, but don't tolerate disrespect.

MOVEMENT

You have by now probably reached the limits of how long students can sit quietly without doing something. One of the functions, actually, of the student who acts out is to serve as an alarm clock to let you know that it is time to change the movement, flow, and energy of the class.

Remember, this is the first day of school after vacation. Students have gotten used to their freedom. Most of them resent being back, stuck inside when the weather is still so nice, and there are so many things they would rather be doing. They've also got a lot on their minds that have little to do with your agenda: which boys or girls they might like, pressures at home, work and other responsibilities, parties coming up. Also, they are just plain tired, not used to getting up so early.

There are a variety of things you can do at this point. You can ask them to fill out information cards, as mentioned in a previous chapter. You could also get them involved in some type of introductory activity with partners or in small groups. You can have them interview each other, with or without guided questions that you have prepared.

Students can be given a list of questions such as the following to ask a partner:

- Where were you born?
- What is your favorite activity outside of school?
- What is your favorite school subject?
- What is your favorite food?
- What kind of music do you like?
- What is your favorite television program?
- What did you do over summer vacation?
- If you could meet anyone in history, who would you choose?
- What do you think is the most difficult job?
- Do you have a nickname you prefer to be called?
- What would you like other people to know about you?
- If you could live anywhere, where would you go?

Another option is to have students participate in a group consensus activity, such as the following:

In groups of four to six people, find examples of the following items that *every* person in the group likes:

- An item of food
- Television program
- Song or musical artist
- Movie
- Personal characteristic in a friend

Still another variation is to organize a scavenger-hunt type of questionnaire that requires students to interact with others in their search for answers. Or you can simply put them in a circle to get them talking. Whatever you do, however, turn the focus on them in such a way that each person gets the chance to speak.

Of the countless techniques teachers have used to encourage students to get to know each other, there is only one that sticks out in my mind. I had a teacher that made up sheets that had about 20 categories. Each category was something like "Find someone in the room that has the same favorite sports team as you" or "Find someone who was born in the same city as you." So each student fills in the worksheet by adding a different student to each category. You can never use the same student twice. There can be rewards for the person that finishes first. This instantly makes the students start talking to one another, and as a result, each person learns something about a fellow classmate.

SETTING THE RULES

Toward the end of the period, draw the students' attention to the topic of class rules. To achieve the goals for the class, some accommodations will have to be made to ensure that the class runs smoothly. Now is the time to review the school rules if you are in a situation where rules for the entire school have been predetermined. If not, you can present the rules you feel are most important. Or, if you choose to be democratic, you can begin discussion with the class and have them give their input on rules. Identify three to five important rules for classroom behavior to simplify your classroom management. Presenting or creating a few specific rules will give you a manageable reference list that can easily be posted for all to see.

One creative variation that is somewhat time-consuming (so you may need to set aside time for it during the second meeting of the class) is to ask the students to work cooperatively in small groups to invent their own rules. Although initially their suggestions may be silly and inappropriate ("We don't need any rules!"), you will be amazed at how wisely they will create exactly the guidelines that are needed. Your job in this exercise is to draw out of them their own commitment to follow rules they develop for themselves. This allows you, at a later time, to be able to say to them, "Look, you are the ones who decided that nobody should be disrespected in this room. I'm just following through on what you came up with."

However rules are explained, you must let students know what behavior is expected and what will happen if they don't follow the guidelines. Be specific and give examples. For instance, if you are bothered by students getting up during the period to sharpen pencils, then tell them, "Pencils should be sharpened before the bell rings. Otherwise, you'll be writing with dull points." Explain the purpose of rules—to meet the needs of students for respect and safety and to promote an academic environment in which learning can occur.

Some Sample Rules

Think of the rule setting as constructive discipline. You are setting up a behavior code that will avoid conflict in the future and provide the students with an environment in which they will be ready to learn. The following examples illustrate the kinds of rules that you might consider implementing. (Again, check your school policies to make sure you are being consistent with them.)

Students should be in their seats when the tardy bell rings. If the tardiness is to be excused or not counted, the student must have a pass. Otherwise, the student must report to the dean's or principal's office.

Homework is due at the beginning of the period. The alternative, of course, is that the students will do it during class and turn it in at the middle or at the end of the period. Some teachers prefer to have the homework turned in or placed in a basket before the tardy bell rings, so that students will concentrate on the lesson and not on finishing their homework.

Covered textbooks are to be brought to class every day. This rule must be stressed, especially for students who come from other countries where procedures may be different. Some schools provide copies for students to keep at home and have a class set available for school use. So, this rule will not be appropriate for all.

Books that are covered remain in better shape and last longer. Also, covers give students an acceptable place to doodle, and the desktops will stay cleaner (we hope). The students can change the book covers to fit their moods. Here's a teaching tip: You can encourage students to put helpful information on the book cover, such as creating time lines for history, or mnemonic devices related to your subject.

Raise your hand and wait to be recognized before speaking. By the secondary level, most students understand the reason for this and are used to the practice of this necessary rule. However, after a break from school, students need to be reminded.

Be courteous and considerate to all students and faculty. Review manners and etiquette. Let students know that swearing will not be tolerated and name-calling is not acceptable. An atmosphere of respect must prevail.

THEORIES AND MODELS OF CLASSROOM DISCIPLINE

There are almost two dozen different models of classroom discipline, each with its own perspective. Although a discussion of classroom management theories is beyond the scope of this book, we feel it is imperative that you give serious thought to your philosophical beliefs on this subject and how you want to manage your classroom. You have already thought about this a lot and discussed it in your education classes. Now is the time to talk to other teachers in your school to find out what has worked best with this particular student population in this specific setting.

Based on your research, develop a policy and practices that are consistent with your beliefs and comfortable for you to implement. The secret is to be proactive rather than to wait for trouble to start. In order to be effective with students, you must be clear and firm. Students will benefit if you provide a supportive structure that is implemented fairly and consistently. When (not if) you experience difficulties, make sure you have given ample time for your selected approach to be implemented before you try another one.

CLASS SYLLABUS

If your class syllabus is available, a logical next step would be to distribute it to your students. If not, at least present the main ideas. First, identify the specific course objectives. Explain the requirements for the class and the evaluation system. The grading scale should be clearly stated. The attendance and makeup procedures should also be carefully explained so as to prevent problems in the future. Set a firm policy on the completion of makeup work and tests. Inform students of your policy on work turned in late. Will it be corrected? Will it be graded? The syllabus sets the framework for the class proceedings. It is worthwhile to commit time and effort to its construction, as it will be read and used by students, parents, and the administration.

GET TO WORK

If there is any time left, start a lesson. Believe it or not, most experienced teachers can get through all the steps mentioned previously and still save some time to address the course content. We are not saying that that is a reasonable expectation for a beginner, but at the very least, be prepared to get into a lesson. By doing so, you will feel reassured that there will be no dead or wasted time.

In your first lesson, be creative and clever. Remember how important first impressions can be. Teach something new that presumes the students have little prior knowledge of the subject (this makes sure everyone is on equal footing). Or, pose a stimulating question related to your subject. Let students leave with something they didn't have when they walked in the door—a new idea, a skill, an interest, a piece of information, an "itch that needs scratching."

ENDING THE PERIOD

Don't let the bell end your class; *you* end it by timing your final words to be spoken before the bell rings. Advise students to leave in an orderly way. Remind them if there is any home-work due. Say goodbye with a smile. Show them you are looking forward to seeing them the next day. Make eye con-tact and say a few words to as many students as you can when they file out of the room. Remember, this is your home during the school day and you want them to feel that way as well.

TIME CONSIDERATIONS

If you are on an abbreviated schedule on the first day of school and your first meeting with the students is a short one, then two adaptations to this plan are suggested. First, wait to review the syllabus until the second day. You may have addi-tional students enrolling after the first day, and they might not appear until the second day anyhow. Second, instead of explaining all the details of class procedures during this brief class period, use a short, get-acquainted activity in which the students work in pairs or in small groups. Your main goal is simply that they will leave their first contact with you saying to themselves (and one another), "Hey, that teacher's pretty cool. That class could be interesting."

A CHEAT SHEET

I (Jeffrey) was so terrified before I taught my first class that I actually wrote out a "cheat sheet" of notes for myself, because I thought for sure I would forget one of the 2,000 different things I wanted to remember. But the idea of bringing notes or an outline with you is a good idea.

The following is a suggested agenda for "Day One:"

Greeting

Say "Good morning" or "Good afternoon."

State your name.

Identify the room and subject.

Introduction of Yourself

Say who you are and where you came from.

Tell about how you came to be a teacher.

Mention your interests related to the subject and outside of school.

Introduction of the Subject

Describe the topics of study.

Mention typical class activities.

Show a sample of projects or products.

Show the textbook.

Introducing the Students to Each Other Through an Activity

Have students introduce themselves and/or share collected information with the class and/or collect written responses.

Class Rules

Discuss the importance of rules.

Present a list or have students develop their own rules.

Distribution of the Syllabus

Go through the syllabus and answer questions students might have regarding grades and assignments.

A Quick Lesson

Briefly engage the students in an activity related to your subject.

Dismissal

Remind students of what they need to be doing before next class. If possible, end on a dramatic note. At the very least, say goodbye in a warm manner.

6

Developing Plans for Instruction and Assessment

"What are we going to do today?" This is often the question that students ask as they come into the classroom. And it is usually followed by, "Will we be doing anything different?" or "Are we having a test today?"

As the instructional leader in the classroom, you need to be ready. Once the students come in and the bell rings, the students' eyes will be on you. It is the moment for you to take charge and commence the learning activities. A well-developed plan will be your guide. It will provide you with your selected objectives for the day, a sequence of activities, a list of needed resources, and assessments. While school districts or principals may request a particular format, there are common elements found in most lesson plans. A general daily lesson plan format follows in Figure 6.1 on page 61, after a short overview discussion on long-term and unit planning.

Long-Term Planning

Take a look at the entire curriculum for which you are responsible and do some preliminary curriculum mapping. This means look at the content standards and decide on the most appropriate sequencing of material. You will also want to estimate how much time will be needed for each topic or content area.

In your planning, note the dates of school vacations, standardized testing, school events, and final exams. This long-range planning gives you a global view of how you will proceed and points out the necessity of keeping a steady pace throughout the year. Most likely there will be adjustments to the plan along the way, but your initial outline will give you a good idea of how to proceed.

You may also be ready at this point to do a textbook correlation, that is, to identify which chapters or sections of chapters in your textbook match the standards. Or, you can examine the content of the textbook as you plan your units.

Unit Planning

Now you are ready to break down the curriculum into units and go into more depth. Integrate concepts or skills together around a topic or theme. If you are using a textbook, you will see how the author or authors have chosen to do this by presenting material in chapter format. The teacher resource books and supplementary materials guides may even provide a number of scope and sequence charts for your consideration, based on the length of your semester. However, you do not have to follow this lead. You can pick and choose material from various chapters for a particular unit. You are not required to have the students tackle the text from "cover to cover." (There is rarely enough time to do so.) Select the information that supports the content standards for your course.

See what supplementary material, such as books or articles, will also support student learning.

Formulate Essential Questions

Today, many educators see the value of structuring learning based on questions. Grant Wiggins and Jay McTighe suggest developing essential questions to engage students and guide their learning. The questions should reflect what you consider to be essential and enduring knowledge, reflect the heart of the discipline, and stimulate discussion. Questions should be open-ended and worded in a way that your students can understand them. By using essential questions, you help students make a personal connection to "the big picture."

With the questions in mind, you can begin to identify the general types of learning experiences you want to provide, the resources you will need, and the best assessments to measure student achievement. For the day-by-day instruction, daily lesson plans are used.

DAILY LESSON PLANS AND ASSESSMENTS

Writing lesson plans serves several functions. The process helps you to organize your thinking about a course, in the short term, for a particular day or week, or in the long term, with a longer unit of study throughout the semester. Developing lesson plans also gives you the opportunity to consider the needs of the particular students in your course as you focus on their prior knowledge, abilities, cultural backgrounds, and levels of English language development in deciding how you will present new material and the forms of assessment you will use to determine if the objectives have been met. Having a set of lesson plans also has the benefit of giving you a sense of confidence as you start the day. It provides an agenda for you and your students to follow. And

Figure 6.1   Lesson Plan Format

Course _____ Period ____ Start & End Times _____ Date _____

Name of Unit _____

Methods _____

Materials/Resources _____

Standard(s):	*National standards, state standards or framework, or district syllabus*
Goal(s):	*Statement of broad direction (may be the same as a standard)*
Related Essential Question(s):	*Open-ended question to guide the learning*
Objective(s):	*Specific statements of measurable outcomes—what students will know or be able to do (may be the same as a standard)*
Assessment(s):	*Informal: checking for understanding, short responses;* *Formal: quiz, end of unit test, project, performance*
Introductory Activity or Anticipatory Set:	*Motivating, engaging brief activity to draw student into the lesson topic*
Body of the Lesson:	*Identification of methods and sequence of activities*
Adaptations and Modifications:	*Considerations for English language learners, special needs populations, struggling readers*
Closure:	*Final activity (summary or reflection) designed to reflect back to the day's objectives and what has been accomplished*
Notes:	*Announcements, homework, "housekeeping activities"*
Reflection:	*Note what worked, what didn't, and why*

if the unexpected situation arises and you are not able to meet your class, such as a last-minute opportunity to attend a professional development activity, an unscheduled meeting, or you become ill, a prepared lesson plan will give the substitute a solid frame of reference.

Basic Information

Begin with the class reference information. Indicate the name of the course, the period, the date, the starting and ending times of the period, and the topic of study. Complete the sections on Methods and Materials/Resources after you have completed the rest of the lesson.

Select the Standard(s)

As most states have adopted content standards or state frameworks, the state standards will be your first reference point. There are also national standards developed for discipline areas that you can access as well. Your district may also have a curriculum in place that incorporates the state standards. These standards identify what students must know and be able to do. Districts may also have a set of benchmarks that identify timelines for meeting the objectives, which you will need to follow.

As the classroom teacher, you will have to do some preliminary inquiry with your students to determine whether they are ready to be introduced to grade-level standards. If not, you may have to incorporate activities based on lower level standards as a preview to the content you want to present.

Formulate Essential Questions

See section above under Unit Plans. If you have not done so earlier, you may want to develop essential questions at this point in your planning.

Goals

Some lesson plan formats include the identification of goals or statements of broad direction that facilitate the designing of curriculum. Goals use such terms as "understand," "appreciate," and "learn." For example: "Students will appreciate the contributions of the impressionist painters." "Students will understand Japanese poetry." They are used for long-term, general planning.

Instructional Objectives

An instructional objective is a statement that defines the outcome or product of instruction in a way that can be measured and observed. It is a subset of a goal. For each content standard, you will need to identify one or more instructional objectives.

Whether you are writing for a daily lesson or a unit of study, the objectives will fall into three categories: cognitive or content; affective or feelings and attitudes; and psychomotor or skills. The emphasis will depend on the course. For example, keyboarding, physical education, band, and art will include many skill objectives; geography and economics will include more cognitive objectives.

In some cases, the objectives will follow a sequence such as in mathematics or language development; in other cases, they may follow a theme such as in social studies. Using Benjamin Bloom's Taxonomy of Thinking Skills as a reference in content areas will ensure that you are including the high-level thinking skills of application, synthesis, and evaluation, as well as the basic skills of knowledge, comprehension, and application.

It is easiest to write objectives using sentences that begin with "The student will . . ." and follow with a verb that indicates performance, such as "define," "identify," "compare," or "solve." You will want to identify something that students can do that you can readily observe, so you can follow their progress. For example: "The student will describe the technique of the impressionist painters." "The student will write a Japanese haiku." Instructional objectives focus on what students will *do*.

At the start of each period, you can then share (orally and by posting on the board or an overhead) the day's objective(s) with students. This not only allows students to know what is expected of them, but also helps them to measure their progress and prepare for tests or other forms of assessment.

Assessment

Now that you have written the objectives, the next step is to decide how you will determine the degree to which students have mastered the objectives. There are two categories of assessment: formative and summative.

Formative assessment takes place during instruction to see if students are progressing. Examples of formative assessment include checking for understanding by monitoring student work as it is completed in class or as homework. You may wish to ask questions as you present new material or demonstrate a new skill to make sure students comprehend what you are talking about or showing. Student responses might also be in the form of showing you answers on individual whiteboards, writing a summary at the end of a period for you to read, completing a graphic organizer that they submit for your review, or taking a quiz.

Summative assessment takes place at the end of a unit. Examples of summative assessment include a unit test or an alternative assessment such as a product (the "proof is in the pudding" in family and consumer sciences) or performance (debating a piece of legislation in government, or playing an instrument in band). You will not be able to use all the various types of assessments for any given unit, but over the course of a semester or year, you can offer students a variety of assessment experiences. Remember, the more different methods you employ, the more different opportunities you give the students to demonstrate their achievements.

Alignment

Assessments need to align with the standards and objectives. They should cover the skills, vocabulary, and content you present. Some teachers also include an item or two from previous units of learning to encourage students to keep reviewing past topics.

Students' responses vary based on the type of assessment they are given. Some students do well on essay tests, but poorly on multiple choice. Since they vary in their ability to perform well on a given type of test item, you will want to provide multiple ways for them to show you what they have learned.

Written Tests

Written objective, "paper and pencil" tests include true/ false, multiple choice, and matching items. Remember, while these types of tests are quick to administer and easy to score, they tend to cover basic information only and depend on students being able to read and comprehend English. They do not measure performance skills or show problem-solving skills.

Tips for creating written test items include the following:

- Using a 12-point font with a type face that is familiar to the students
- Printing on a solid background
- Including all relevant text and graphics on a single page
- Providing clear space for responses
- Listing multiple-choice items vertically
- Avoiding negative words such as "not" or "never"
- Emphasizing words that are significant, such as "never" or "always" by putting them in italics or boldface type
- When using fill-in-the-blank questions, placing blanks at the end of the sentence ("The capital of the United States is _____.")
- Selecting choice items that are the same length, shorter then the introductory stem, and include plausible answers

- Having only one right answer
- Using the same vocabulary as used during instruction

Make sure as much of your content as possible is included in the items. Students expect to be tested on all the content presented. If you use publisher-created tests, check to see that the above guidelines have been followed. Many schools have scantron forms available to score such tests electronically. This type of testing will also give students practice for standardized testing.

Fill-in-the-blank and open-ended, short-answer questions will take more time to grade, but will give you a fuller picture of what students know. They provide students with the opportunity to use their own words, identify examples, and give analogies. There may be a variety of correct responses to open-ended questions.

Special-needs students and English-language learners will need modifications of the test and adaptations of procedures in order to be successful on these types of items. Depending on their abilities, you may choose to provide word banks, select fewer items, and/or include samples of correctly answered items.

Essay questions are closely tied to students' writing skills and ability to communicate. Therefore, they may be difficult for special-needs and English-language learners. Again, modifications and adaptation may be needed. Because it is more difficult to cover all the content with essay tests, many teachers use a combination of items. Grading essays takes a long time, but using rubrics (see page 68) will help you do so efficiently and reliably.

Alternative Assessments

By using alternative assessments (see Box 6.1), you allow students to give you a fuller picture of their achievement. Alternative assessments are also greatly appealing to students. They can involve a performance or demonstration, such as a

---

BOX 6.1   LIST OF ALTERNATIVE ASSESSMENTS

Advertisement, artifact replicas, animated stories
Brochure
Collage, children's book
Dance, debate, demonstration, diorama, drawings
Editorial
Fashion show
Games
Historical portrayal of person or event
Interview
Journal entry
K-W-L Chart
Letter, learning log
Maps, mobiles, models, movie, museum
Newscast
Obituary
Photographic essay, play, poem, political cartoon, poster
Questionnaire and results analysis, quilt
Role play
Simulation, slide show, song, speech, storyboard
Television program, think-aloud
Unit summary with illustrations
Video documentary, virtual field trip
Web site, word wall
Xylograph-wood engraving or other artistic rendering
Yearbook or similar type documentary
Z to A or A to Z alphabet-type presentation

---

dance; or a presentation, such as a PowerPoint slide show of a research project or a speech; or a product, such as a ceramic bowl, or a newspaper created by hand or by using Publisher software. Whatever the assignment, alternative assessments involve a lot of time and preparation to implement, and performances and presentations take time to evaluate.

Rubrics

Checklists, rating scales, or rubrics facilitate the evaluation process. By using rubrics or scoring guides with writing assignments, you identify the characteristics of a project or performance that will be graded and how the grade will be determined. Both students and parents appreciate such detailed information. The mystery is taken out of grading as it becomes more objective. Students can be involved in creating the rubrics and can self-evaluate their work based on what has been developed. Scoring can be holistic or analytic. You will also find that rubrics enable you to grade student work more quickly. In both types of rubrics, you would include the skills and knowledge pertinent to the unit.

Holistic Scoring

A holistic rubric gives an overall picture by grouping together the characteristics being evaluated. A continuum of proficiency is developed from high to low and a point value assigned to each category. Figure 6.2 is a general example of a holistic scoring guide. A score is given according to the category that best matches the quality of the work. With such a guide, students know exactly what is expected. Teachers can quickly give feedback to the students, but it tends to be general rather than specific in nature.

Analytic Scoring

Analytic scoring gives points for specific criteria. (See Figure 6.3.) It therefore gives more detailed feedback to the students. The criteria may or may not be grouped in categories. Points are totaled for a grade.

Introductory Activity

After your goals, essential questions, objectives, and assessments have been determined, you are ready to plan

Figure 6.2   General Example of Holistic Scoring Guide

3	The information in the project is accurate. There are three or more visuals to support the text in the project. The project incorporates standard English grammar and usage with no mistakes.
2	The information in the project is correct with minor errors. There are one or two visuals to support the text in the project. The project incorporates standard English grammar and usage with some mistakes.
1	The information in the project is inaccurate. There are no visuals to support the text in the project. The project has many mistakes in standard English grammar and usage.

There are 3 points possible using this rubric. Additional criteria can be added to each level as desired.

Figure 6.3   General Example of Analytic Scoring Guide

Criteria/ Points	3	2	1
Information	Accurate	Generally correct, one to three errors	Inaccurate, many mistakes
Visuals to support text	3 visuals to support text	2 visuals to support text	0-1 visual to support text
Standard English grammar and usage	Complete sentences with no spelling or grammatical errors	Generally complete sentences, with a few spelling and/or grammatical errors	Incomplete sentences with spelling and/or grammatical errors

There are 9 points possible using this guide. Other criteria to consider include organization, use of references, creativity, presentation, and neatness.

the lesson. Whether you have a traditional 45- to 55-minute period, or a block session that is longer, you will want to start with an introductory activity that is engaging and motivating. Effective introductions link to prior knowledge and stimulate the senses. You can use art, music, video, poetry, quotes, present an interesting question, or perform a brief demonstration. Movement is also important since children, much more than adults, get impatient with sitting still.

When I (Jeffrey) was teaching a lesson with Bushman children in Namibia, I quickly learned that anything we did together had to take place within a context of movement, whether that involved pantomime, dance, or exercise. My first thought was that in this so-called primitive culture, the children had never learned the skills of what it takes to be successful students. Then I realized that in our culture, we have actually unlearned the skills of what it takes to have fun while learning. The whole idea of learning by sitting motionless in seats while being talked to is antithetical to everything we know and understand about how learning takes places. The more active we can structure our lessons, the more likely that students will remain truly engaged.

Above all else, the introductory activity should be designed to capture student attention and set the stage for the day's lessons. This opening activity is sometimes referred to as the "anticipatory set." It should be followed with a statement of objectives and explanation of why this is important. Then you are ready to proceed.

Note: Many teachers begin the period with a "bellringer" or an initial "sponge" activity to get students involved as soon as the bell rings. This activity may or may not be related to the lesson of the day. A review "question of the day," "warm-up" problem, or the copying of objectives and homework assignment, all of which are not related to the lesson and do not serve a motivating purpose, should not be considered as an introductory activity. We suggest listing these activities under the "Notes" section of the lesson plan.

Learning Activities

The body of the lesson follows. Now, you select the methods (for example, direct instruction, inquiry, or cooperative learning) and identify the corresponding activities for students, including time to practice what they have learned. Remember to consider learning styles as well as multiple intelligences in order to give students the opportunity to function in their areas of preference and strength, as well as to give exposure to and build confidence in their less-preferred and weaker areas. Some teachers try to estimate how much time each activity will take, structuring time for students to practice individually and in groups under their guidance. Include time for cleaning up material and supplies and putting books and resources away. Don't forget to list the supplementary materials and supplies you will need in the "Materials/ Resources" section of the lesson plan. With this list in hand, you will be able to gather quickly the items you need for the period. Some teachers like to list the Web sites they will access if using the Internet during class.

Adaptations and Modifications

Given the mix of students' English language development, reading abilities, and cultural backgrounds, lessons need to be differentiated when and where it is possible to accommodate the various learners in the classroom. Moreover, reading strategies need to be incorporated into each class.

- *Special-Needs Students.* This population of students will have Individualized Education Plans (IEPs) indicating modifications and adaptations to be made for those who qualify. Some of the changes you may need to implement include the following: breaking assignments into small chunks, using graphic organizers, narrowing the focus to key terms and concepts, allowing extra time for completion of tasks, using a computer or other

Figure 6.4   Brief Overview of Language Development
Proficiency Levels and Student Characteristics With
Corresponding Teacher Strategies

Level of Proficiency Language Proficiency	Student Characteristics	Teacher Strategies
Level 1: Preproduction	Recognizes words Uses nonverbal responses	Use gestures with speech, pictures, models, demonstrations
Level 2: Early Production	Understand main ideas Repeats words heard frequently	Build on student knowledge Ask who, what, where, when questions
Level 3: Beginning Speech	Initiates conversations Mispronounces words Expands vocabulary	Introduce reading and writing Correct speech in context
Level 4: Intermediate Fluency	Uses longer sentences Begins to think in English	Provide opportunity to use language Ask open-ended questions
Level 5: Advanced Fluency	Produces written and oral language	Focus on reading and writing skills

assistive technologies, having someone else write for
them. Their assessments will have to be similarly
modified. Each student will have an IEP, which will
give you guidance.

- *English-Language Learners.* These students present their
own challenges. It may be helpful to look at the level of
language ability and then design activities and assessments accordingly. A brief overview of five levels of language proficiency, characteristics of students, and a few
corresponding suggested teacher strategies are found in
Figure 6.4.

Figure 6.5   Literacy Strategies

Graphic Organizers: Use before, during, and after reading, such as time lines, Venn diagrams, cause and effect charts, outlines
KWL: Have students identify what they **K**now, what they **W**ant to know and then at the end of the study, what they have **L**earned
Pictures, objects, models: Use to give students a visual reference for what they will be reading about
SQ3-R: Survey, Question, Read, Recite, Review with text
Textbook Scavenger Hunts: Use to acquaint students with texts at the beginning of the year
Vocabulary Cards: Use with picture references, definitions
Word Walls: Create a bank of related vocabulary on a bulletin board

The assessments for English-language learners will also require changes. You may decide to include a word bank and/or allow for drawings or other visual representations, outlines, or graphic organizers.

- *Grouping.* Some children enjoy working in groups, while others like to work alone. Different groupings should be facilitated. You may want to assign group members based on their diversity and learning needs or you may decide to have homogeneous groups and change group membership periodically so that all students have a chance to work with and get to know each other.

For some activities, the class may participate as a whole; for other activities, partner work may be most appropriate; and a third structure is to have students work individually. Or, you can use a combination with differentiated learning, that is, having students work on different tasks related to a given objective according to their abilities. This is an effective way of meeting the needs of all students in your class. In particular, it provides a structure for gifted students to work on challenging content at their own pace.

Teaching Reading

With the *No Child Left Behind* emphasis on literacy, all teachers need to be responsible for developing literacy skills. The literacy strategies listed in Figure 6.5 will help get you started.

Carefully selected supplementary reading material will often capture students' attention and engage them on a given topic, where students often get lost in the monotony of textbooks.

Students often fail to see the practical value of what they are reading. I (Cary) remember thinking all the time, "What does this stuff have to do with anything?" or "Why will I ever need to know about this?" Well, my Government teacher had a unique solution to combat this problem. She had each of the students in her class get a subscription to Newsweek magazine. They offered a student rate so it wasn't very expensive. Each week we were required to read the articles relating to American and world politics. We took a short quiz each Friday on how the articles related to the areas of government we were studying at the time. Not only was it more fun and interesting to read than the textbook, it also let us know what was going on in the world.

Closure

At the end of the period, take a few minutes to relate the learning activities back to the objectives. This can take place in the form of a brief summary (such as a whole-class, small-group, or partner discussion), or writing a reflection (such as a journal response in which students contemplate what they learned or experienced during the period), or a culminating activity that demonstrates mastery (such as integrating new vocabulary or performing a new skill).

Notes

At the beginning or at the end of the period, there may be various "housekeeping" activities you may want to list. Such items might include general school announcements and attendance at the beginning of the period, and directions for homework and other reminders related to your class at the end of the period.

Reflection

It is a good idea to spend some time reflecting each day after class to evaluate how the class went as compared to the plan. Some questions to ask yourself might include the following:

- How did the students respond to the introductory activity? Did they become engaged? Did it serve the inspirational or motivational purpose you intended?
- Were students able to progress successfully through the lesson? If not, what obstacles can you identify?
- How was the pacing? Too fast? Too slow? Just right?
- Were there any materials or references that should have been included?
- Were there any questions that the students asked that could have been addressed differently?
- Was the sequencing appropriate?
- Did students need additional scaffolding?
- What other changes would you make in the future? Is there anything you would do differently?

INTEGRATING INPUT FROM TESTING

At some point, and hopefully sooner rather than later, you will receive additional information on your students to help you with your planning. As the data from standardized testing become available, the results will be given to you. *Criterion-referenced tests* are designed to measure what students have learned against a set of standards (criteria) such as the district objectives. They are locally developed. The tests you give at the end of a semester, for example, will likely be criterion-referenced tests. Your district may have course exit exams. This type of test tells you whether or not your students have mastered identified objectives. You receive specific feedback from this kind of evaluation. You will see how well your students did in the past and whether any gaps exist that you will need to address. This information on your students will enable you to identify areas for re-teaching.

The other type of information you will receive is from the *norm-referenced tests* that are receiving much national attention. (They are being used as the basis for school accountability.) These tests measure students against like students, usually across the nation. For example, the achievement of a second-semester, 11th-grade student in your school is compared to all second-semester, 11th-grade students who took the test. You will receive information on how students did on various tasks included in the test; however, information from the task analysis tends to be general rather than specific. Also, these tests are highly dependent on reading ability, which can be a problem. Unfortunately, there is often a lag time of weeks or months between the date the test is submitted for scoring and the date the received results are shared with teachers.

FINAL THOUGHTS ON PLANNING

We encourage you to be as thorough as time permits in writing your initial lesson plans. For some activities, you will want to be very complete, perhaps even scripting what you want to say. For other activities, a brief outline will suffice. You may be able to follow a lesson plan from another source, such as the teacher's resource kit for your textbook, a plan you received from another teacher, or one you found on the Internet. Sometimes you will be able to attach an already-developed lesson to the form you use; however, most likely you will have to make adjustments for your students. As time goes on, you will become more efficient in developing your plans.

7

Managing Time and Paperwork

A nd you thought teaching was mostly about direct instruction and interactions with students. If only that were so.

Secondary school teachers are besieged with paperwork, and you had better organize yourself from the beginning or you will feel like you will never catch up. There are daily attendance rosters to manage, not to mention reports to various offices, lesson plans to write in which you pretend to know what you might end up doing in the future, homework assignments to read and check off, papers to evaluate, tests to create and grade—the list goes on and on.

We don't mean to be discouraging, just realistic. Paperwork doesn't have to get you down if you are well-organized, efficient, and sensible in the ways you operate.

ATTENDANCE

Your attendance book is a legal document and can be subpoenaed by a court of law. It takes a few minutes each day and must be attended to with care. One teacher we know videotapes his classes, one student at a time, as they say their names and something brief about themselves. He then studies the tape on his own time, drilling himself to memorize names. Students are thus *very* impressed that he can take attendance after the first few days simply by scanning the room. Teachers with digital cameras can quickly take pictures and print them on seating charts to help them learn their students' names.

Another unique way to take attendance is with a specially designed board in the front of the room. Each student has an assigned magnet that is kept in a column up on the board. As students enter the room each day, they see a question written on the board with several possible answers. These questions can relate to the subject matter or even be more playful, as the following examples show:

The question: What is your favorite fast food?

The choices: pizza, hamburgers, tacos

The question: Where is the Nile River located?

The choices: Asia, Africa, Antarctica, Australia

Each day, you would make up a different question for students to consider as they enter the room. They would then remove their individual magnets and place them in one of the columns. The names leftover are those who are absent. You can even begin class with a discussion of the question that you asked. Remember, it is your responsibility to check that the magnets accurately reflect who is present in your class.

GRADES

As a classroom teacher, you will frequently receive requests for students' grades, whether it is from a counselor, a parent, a dean, or the student. In a formal way, many secondary schools send out progress reports indicating "unsatisfactory progress" midway through a reporting period. Athletic and activity (spirit leader, band) eligibility checks take place regularly, too. Therefore, it is very important to have the grading up to date. For this purpose, a computer grading program is strongly recommended. Programs such as MicroGrade are easy to use and compute the averages as soon as grades are entered into the computer. You can even e-mail messages or grade reports to an individual student or to everyone in the class.

The computer programs are flexible and allow you to designate your columns based on whatever categories you prefer (participation, class work, homework, projects, quizzes, tests) and whatever weighting system you choose (points, percentages). They will even compute extra-credit work into the average. Furthermore, if you have access to a printer, the programs allow you to immediately print a report of a student's grades very quickly. It is helpful to have this information for reports on students that you submit to athletic directors or other administrators or parents on request.

Some districts now allow teachers to use printouts of the computer pages as formal records rather than complete traditional grade books by hand. Also, some districts will provide grading programs for you, so check before you buy your own.

Most teachers are still required to turn in a traditional grade book. These books are designed in such a way that very small lines run horizontally, in sets of two or three, across the page. This works fine if all you are doing is keeping attendance, as you can easily use one line for each student.

Although the lines may be numbered, I (Ellen) ignore the printed numbers. On the top line, I print the student's name and mark attendance. Then, I use the next two (or three or more depending on how many categories I have) for grades. For example, the second line is used for test and quiz grades. The third line is used for homework and class work. On the fourth line, I keep a running average of each student's overall grade for the reporting period, and notes to myself to indicate places and people the student visited other than my class (such as a field trip, or the nurse's or dean's office). It is too hard to squeeze all the information in on one line, so I try to be creative in my use of a traditional grade book. The advantage of this system is that when a student is missing a grade, you can quickly see if it was due to negligence or due to an absence. Some schools will require a page for attendance only and subsequent pages for grades. In that case, you may have to adjust your record keeping.

Students can be taught to keep track of their own grades and compute their own averages. You need to explain the weighting system and give examples. Many teachers provide forms for the students to use throughout the card-marking period. You may want to have parents sign to indicate they have seen these forms and are aware of their child's progress in your class.

PAPERWORK CONSIDERATIONS

One of the major mistakes common to beginning teachers is giving too many written assignments. Remember: You are making as much work for yourself as you are for your students. Each paper or assignment must be read, evaluated, graded, recorded, and then the grade must be averaged. All of this can be very time-consuming, and some of you may wish to have some sort of life outside of school.

There are a number of things you can consider as ways to reduce your workload:

Always consider the merit of the assignment. Is it really necessary in order to accomplish the larger goals you are after? There is nothing that turns students off more than busy work in which they can't see how it will help them in some constructive way.

Can the assignment be self-graded or self-evaluated? Because the purpose of many assignments is to give students systematic practice in new concepts and skills and then to integrate feedback into their future learning, there is no reason

why you have to be the one who does all the evaluating. Post the correct answers on the board, and let students review their own answers. Occasionally, you can spot-check for accuracy, with warnings that if students make too many mistakes in their self-corrections, they will lose all credit.

Can you use a scantron machine to score the assessment? Using scantrons will be a great time-saver. The forms are available in many sizes, and some have space available for essay questions. Students, especially younger ones, need opportunities to "bubble" their responses as practice for standardized tests.

Can the assignment be completed as a group or paired activity? This is one way to cut the number of papers you have to grade in half. Students may also benefit from the cooperative effort, assuming they each participate equally.

Does the assignment need to be graded at all? Sometimes, feedback (such as constructive comments and corrections) is all that is needed. A grade may not be necessary.

It isn't always necessary to collect homework assignments each day. Sometimes, a weekly or biweekly homework check may be sufficient, in which case the students are responsible for maintaining their own paperwork.

Control the length of the assignments to fall within reasonable limits. Do this both for the students' benefit and to manage your own available time. Students may not need to write an essay, when they can provide an outline or concept map of ideas to show they have mastered an objective.

Vary the type of assignments and evaluation methods you use. Do this not only to give students a chance to demonstrate different skills, but also to create variety for yourself.

Rather than just requiring written assignments, be creative.
Design performance or project assignments that can show
mastery of the material. Students can create dioramas, plays,
posters, or videos. This will benefit those whose learning
strengths are other than writing and those learning English.

Share the load. An interdisciplinary approach might have
one teacher evaluate an assignment for content (e.g., science,
social studies) while another evaluates for technical writing
skills (English).

Use aides, if available. Many schools provide student aides
for teachers. Often, you will be able to create assignments that
the aides can correct, if not grade. With the use of computer
grading programs, aides, if permitted, can be taught to enter
grades on the computer for quick averaging.

Use rubrics. Create your own rubric or have students create
rubrics for scoring. This way, students know before they begin
an assignment what the criteria will be for evaluation. Rubrics
will allow you to quickly assess student work.

**Decide on the best time for you to examine student assign-
ments.** Some teachers are able to get most of their work done
during preparation periods. Others remain in their rooms
after school so they can go home without anything else to
worry about. Still others prefer to relax for a while and complete their paperwork at night or early in the morning.
Whatever structure you prefer, stick with a consistent program so you are able to keep on top of things.

Be punctual in returning assignments to students. Remember
that you are modeling appropriate work habits. Always do
what you say you will do, if you expect your students to do
the same.

I (Cary) remember one time how hard I worked for a certain grade in math class. Needing an "A" to achieve a good grade for the quarter, I spent countless hours reviewing the material. After taking the test, I turned it in to the teacher confidently. As my next math class approached, I got really excited waiting to get my test back. I really needed that reward to keep my momentum going because the next lesson was really hard.

I showed up for class the next day and was surprised the teacher said nothing about returning our tests. When I asked him what was going on, he said he'd have them ready the next day. Again I waited not so patiently, and again the same thing happened. A whole week went by, and still we never got the tests back. Finally, I got up the nerve to ask the teacher again; this time, he yelled at me to stop bugging him.

About a week and a half after taking the test, we finally got the test back, and I received my A. But it didn't seem to matter any more. We were already on to other stuff, and I cut back on my study time because I had no idea how I was doing in the class.

When kids work hard for tests, they deserve to get their grades back as soon as possible. Whatever you do, don't lie by telling them they'll have their tests back within 2 days and not give them back for a week. If you are going to have problems grading the tests right away, tell the kids so they will know what to expect. Better yet, get the grades back to us as soon as you can. We need to know how we're doing in your classes.

The Mailbox

Along with the things you initiate for your students to complete will be paperwork required by the school. Some days, it will seem impossible to keep your mailbox empty.

Every time you go by, there will be something in it for you to peruse—announcements, requests for information, forms to fill out, plus the countless catalogues and letters from text and instructional materials companies. It's a good idea to check your mailbox frequently—before and after school, during lunch, and at other times during the day if possible.

In the beginning, it is wise to look carefully at the papers that are placed in your mailbox. Once you become familiar with the types of information you receive, you will be able to categorize and prioritize your responses. Daily announcements will be stuffed in mailboxes every day, usually at about the same time. Scan these for the information that pertains to you or your students. You can post an announcement of a forthcoming assembly (with the bell schedule for that day) on the class bulletin board for reference later in the week. College visits and college scholarship announcements can also be posted, in addition to competitions and performances that are coming up. Each day, you can refer your students to the latest additions to the bulletin board. Telephone messages from parents and messages from other teachers will be placed in your mailbox, too, another reason to check your box regularly.

Take a pen with you to the mailbox. Often there will be a request for information that you can provide on the spot. Such requests are very common at the beginning of the year as administrators check on the numbers of students, textbooks, desks, and other equipment. These forms are often placed in the mailboxes in the morning and usually require a quick turnaround time—the end of the school day. Also, there will be information sheets to be posted—fire drill procedures suspension rules, reminders about no food or drink in the classroom, and the like. The good news is that the amount of paperwork in your mailbox will decrease as time goes on. If you have a writing tool with you, you can process some of the paper and send it on its way.

Advertising catalogues, brochures, and flyers will find their way to you. It will take a little while in the beginning to sort through the new products that are being offered. But as time goes on, you will be able to determine which companies have books or products that are worth your consideration for a particular course. File the catalogues by class or by publisher until you are in a position to request an order. You will also get information on various programs and competitions that you and your students may be interested in, as well as information on professional development opportunities. Check with other teachers and your department head for their opinions on the information you receive.

PLANNING AND CALENDARS

Just as students are advised to use daily planners in study-skills classes, we suggest that a calendar or electronic planner (personal data assistant—PDA) will be helpful to you as well. Such a planner is useful for keeping track of scheduled meetings, student activities, and deadlines for various projects. You can color code entries to distinguish between professional and personal entries, and you can indicate optional activities, such as attending a debate in which one of your students will be participating. You can also include reminders for forthcoming events.

IN THE BEGINNING

The early weeks of the fall semester will be especially busy with the first department and school committee meetings of the year. There will be several tasks that must be completed right away; for example, an individual and department professional development plan may need to be written. Most schools require these to be submitted to an administrator. Emergency lesson plans may have to be written and filed as well. Once they are completed, they must also be updated from time to time. Also, texts and supplies will need to be inventoried and stored, at least temporarily. And, forms—well, this topic merits a section of its own.

FORMS

Certain forms are distributed on a regular basis. You can mark your calendar so you know when to expect them and when they are due back to a particular office. For example, athletic and activity eligibility forms are distributed on a regular schedule and are due back by a specific time. Some schools require these every week; others may only want them every third week.

In order to evaluate eligibility for sports and activities, some teachers make a notation in their grade books as to which students play a given sport or participate in a given activity. Then, they scan the list of names and check the grade averages for those students. Other teachers find this information distracting in the grade books, so they circle the names on the lists that are given to each teacher and just check the circled names against the grade averages in their grade books.

Unsatisfactory progress report forms are distributed at some point in the middle of the grading period. Teachers usually have several days to complete them. You can check the due dates, usually with the registrar or the principal's secretary. Progress reports may also be requested for certain students on a weekly basis. These forms may come from the student, parent, counselor, special education teacher, dean, school social worker, or school psychologist.

Some schools have teachers complete daily attendance rosters. The forms are in the mailboxes in the morning and have to be turned in at the end of the day. Suspension lists and withdrawals are posted daily. The teacher usually has a part in the withdrawal process—checking in textbooks and indicating withdrawal in the grade book, which is a legal document. You may also have to sign a form. A good procedure to follow is to check the lists against your record book at the end of the day before you turn in your attendance.

Excused-absence lists are irregularly distributed, so you have to be on the lookout for these. Students may be excused for competitions, assembly preparation, sports events, field trips, and other programs. In addition, several tests are administered throughout the year for different groups of students. You might consider marking these on your calendar, too, so you will know why students are absent.

ORGANIZE YOUR WORK SPACE

Take a moment to analyze your work habits and your work space. Is your desk rather cluttered at the moment with papers, folders, and books? Or, have you seen the advantages to clearing your desk except for the current project?

Think of your work space in terms of zones. Keep the items you use regularly; by that we mean daily, in the immediate vicinity—on or in your desk. Items that fall into this category include textbooks, confidential information, grade book, lesson plans, paper and pens, and desk supplies kept in a drawer. If you are not going to use it right away, it probably doesn't have to be on your desk.

Reference items such as the Teacher Handbook, dictionary, and curriculum resource materials should be placed in an intermediate zone, within arm's reach, such as in or on a nearby bookshelf or table. If you must have piles of papers and materials, and some of us do, request or bring in an extra table so that you will be able to see what you have accumulated. This way you will be able to spread out your papers and still have a place to work.

Decide in advance where students will put their completed work so you will have access to it. Will they place it in a basket on a table on the side of the room or file it in a drawer? Where will they find their makeup work—in a basket, on the bulletin board, or in a file cabinet? Also, determine how you will return their work—will they have mailboxes or folders for retrieval or will you hand papers back personally? Establishing routines will make your life and your students' lives easier.

Things you use from time to time, such as class sets of supplies or supplementary reading or folders/binders of resource plans, can be stored out of the way in cabinets, wardrobes, or bookshelves on the side or in the back of the room.

Decide whether you will keep lesson plans, lectures, transparencies, and other information in folders or binders; or experiment to find out which is most comfortable for you. We suggest color coding your files, binders, and boxes for easy reference. It goes without saying, keep like materials together.

Space may be an issue in two particular situations. If you travel from room to room, you will only be able to bring what is essential with you on a cart. You will have to be extremely selective in your choosing. Carts have weight limits and can tip over if they are unbalanced. Also, it is difficult to maneuver a cart with objects that extend over the sides in hallways full of students. You will have to find a place for your reference books and supplementary materials, supplies, and student work. You might store them in a department office or in a room shared with another teacher.

If you inherited a room from another teacher, you may find the cabinets full of real or imagined treasures. You may want to box these items for storage elsewhere until you have time to go through them and decide what will be useful for you and what you can discard.

Managing Time

Some days when school ends, you may feel totally overwhelmed, as if you put out one fire after another all day long. When you consider the next day's work, you don't know where to begin.

There's no denying your days will be very full, and each day will be different from the day before. In order to manage your time efficiently, the first step is to create your "TTD" or "Things To Do" list. Next to each item on the list, it is also helpful to identify what resources you will need to accomplish each task. In some cases, you will need to gather additional information or consult with someone else. Sometimes, you can even predict how long each task will take (just as you do with lesson plans). For example, you may identify several short items to do regularly during your preparation period, such as grading and recording makeup work. Other items you may do on a weekly basis, such as getting supplies or calling parents. Examine your list to determine which things need to be done right away, which items within a week, and which have later deadlines. Then prioritize your work and set a schedule for yourself for other things that must be done— personal shopping, dentist appointments, and so on.

It's important to set realistic deadlines. There are only 24 hours in a day and you need to sleep, eat, exercise, and spend time with your family and friends. Remember, too, to ask for help when you need it. Other teachers may have models for you to follow and suggestions that will help you do things efficiently. A mentor can also help you prioritize your tasks.

There will be many requests and opportunities for involvement at the school, from coaching sports to advising clubs to curriculum development. You will enjoy these commitments, but they also take time. You may have to remind people several times that you are a new teacher, and that while you would like to get more involved, you are not ready to do so at the present. Target what you would like to do and put it on the list for next year!

AT THE END

It's hard to believe, with everything you are trying to remember as you're just getting started in the job, but there will come a time when the academic year ends. Unfortunately, this brings another rash of forms to fill out and paperwork to complete.

At the end of each semester, you will need to post schedules for final exams. There will be forms for you to fill out regarding your preferences for teaching next year, textbook needs and supplies, and maintenance requests for your room over the track or summer. Various evaluation forms also will be requested.

Teachers with senior students will have to report semester grades and fines. They may be involved in distributing graduation-related material, such as senior rings, caps and gowns, and invitations. This is the time for recommendations, resumes, and senior projects. Do not agree to review a resume or write a letter of recommendation if the student does not give you enough time to do so—at least a week.

All of this paperwork may seem overwhelming in the beginning. It is really just during the first few weeks and the last few weeks of the year that things seem particularly hectic. Before you become frustrated, remember that almost all professional jobs in contemporary life have their fair share of forms and paperwork to complete. You will become more efficient as time goes on. This is just the price we pay for the privilege of doing the fun stuff.

8

Avoiding Boredom— Theirs and Yours

If there's one thing that kids hate most about school (besides having to get up early), it's the boredom. I (Cary) think that most teachers are so repetitive and predictable. Whether it's taking notes or doing problems on the board, the same routines are used over and over again.

My advice is: Avoid this! Take risks by trying new ideas. If students come to class and they already know they're going to be lectured to all period, then interest is lost before things even begin.

The way to get my attention (and keep me from falling asleep) is to surprise me. Be innovative and enthusiastic. Catch me off guard, and I will respond positively. Last of all, never act like you are bored. When I can see my teacher is bored, it is definitely going to rub off on me.

The following situation seems to happen too often. I walk into my science classroom, passing a hanging skeleton and all the usual posters of plants and animals. The bell rings, and I take my seat. Well, first I talk to a few of my friends.

The teacher takes attendance and then walks over to the light switch, turning it off. You can hear groans across the room. He turns the overhead projector on and begins the usual hour of nonstop talking. The classroom is dark and stuffy. In the background, I hear the teacher's monotone explaining something. What was that he just said? My head droops, and I feel the coolness of the table against my face. I'm drifting away.

I'm sorry, but in that situation, I really couldn't care less whether a fish has a three-chambered heart or a four-chambered heart.

Who cares?

Entering my history class after lunch, I notice my teacher is not in the room. Every day, I look forward to this class as my teacher makes the past come alive. The bell rings and still no teacher. A friend and I start talking about the fight that happened at lunch, as do most of my other class-mates. Suddenly, the door is whisked open, and my usually jovial teacher enters with a sullen look on his face.

"Everybody, shut up right now!" he yells.

There is complete silence.

Now, this is weird. This teacher never yells at us. A girl starts to giggle, and my teacher screams at her, "Get out of this classroom right now!"

During the next several minutes, two more kids are thrown out of the classroom for the dumbest reasons—one is chewing gum; the other has forgotten her pen. He screams at the gum chewer, who is on the verge of tears: "Get out of here! The gum always ends up on the floor."

As the teacher paces the room, none of us are even breathing. We are terrified, as much by how strange this is as by how cruel he is being to us. The teacher walks to the door, opens it, and directs all the students in the hallway (there are now 7 or 8 of them by then) to go to the dean's office. Then he goes back to his desk and asks someone a question that nobody knows the answer to. He storms out of the room claiming he can't teach kids who are as stupid as we are.

We all sit there in silence, wondering what happened to our wonderful teacher. A few minutes later, he enters the room, bringing all of the kids back. Strangely, he has his usual smile on his face. What the heck is going on?

The teacher explains that what he was doing was acting out the role of a dictator. We had been studying World War II and learning about the ways Hitler and Mussolini had been able to control the populace. The rest of the period, we are so charged up about what we had experienced that none of us want to leave when the bell rings. Now, that is teaching!

What Cary described in the first example is typical of what so many children experience in school. It isn't that they aren't interested in learning, it's just that they don't want to learn what you are teaching or at least in the way you are presenting the material to them. All human beings learn best when they are actively engaged with the content as Cary shows in the second example, when they see the relevance of the subject to their lives, when they can imagine specific ways that investing their time and energy will result in something useful and practical. Your job, then, is to keep the children, and yourself, excited about what is going on in your classroom. Find a connection that relates to them personally.

CAPTURING AND MAINTAINING INTEREST

Long-term planning will help you see the picture of what students experience in the classroom. Take note of your usual teaching methods and look for new methods and/or novel introductory activities to kick off a unit. Using a variety of instructional methods and assessments will provide you and your students with needed stimulation. Let the multiple intelligences mentioned in Chapter 3 be your guide. Include art, music, poetry, and movement in your lessons. Reach your students on an emotional level. Involve them in collaborative projects. Encourage them to take risks and try new roles or ways of thinking. The following list suggests several ways to fan the flames of interest.

Challenge the students to become actively involved. They can develop interviews, plays, or simulations of events. If you haven't seen students act out the firing of a neuron, you've got a sight to see! They can produce projects such as journals, books, newspapers, displays, or products to show you results of their research. Ask them to write a jingle, an advertisement, or a song. For example, students in Spanish can demonstrate a conversation between a student and a counselor. Math students can role-play the use of an algebra problem in a real-world setting. History students can make a magazine of events about a cultural issue. Child development students can create a poster to demonstrate safety issues for toddlers. Home economics students can plan a restaurant and create a menu. Geography students can write songs to describe environments and cultures they have studied. Students teach each other. You facilitate the learning by providing resources and direction, and feedback as needed. Students with limited English language skills tend to be more comfortable working in small-group situations. Their peers with help them learn new words and use them fluently.

Stimulate higher level student thinking. Teach higher order thinking skills. Ask open-ended questions. Pose situations or problems in which students will have to analyze, synthesize, and evaluate information individually and in small groups. Groups can present the results of their discussion to the whole class. Use the "What if" scenario to get them thinking. Give students plenty of time to formulate answers.

Be dramatic. If you are comfortable doing so, you can exaggerate your tone of voice and gestures for emphasis. Use your voice to its greatest potential. Learn a magic trick if it will spur interest. Dress in a costume to create an effect. Demonstrate your passion for your subject.

Decorate. Change your room. Rearrange the furniture. Create new bulletin boards that correspond to the current topic of study. Turn your room into a museum by bringing in artifacts or pictures. Use your wall space and boards to create a setting in which students will be involved in a project. Hang signs from the ceiling. Bring in lamps to change the lighting. Just create a new atmosphere of the unexpected so that students begin to wonder what will happen next.

Illustrate your subject. Use diagrams, pictures, slides, models. Create your own art work. Use charts. Make cartoons. Show photographs. Bring in samples. Play music. Show movies. Do demonstrations and create models. These visual aids are especially important in working with language learners. These students are often familiar with the concepts you are discussing, but may not recognize the terms you use. The visuals create a common basis for all students. Students with disabilities will also benefit from the visual references.

Instigate questions. Bring in a big box or a big bag, and clear away the space around it. Put a question mark on the front. Let the students guess what is in it. Surprise them with an interesting artifact. Use inquiry as a method of teaching.

Inscribe thought-provoking quotes. Questions or statements can be posed for students' reactions. They can serve as the basis of a journal entry, a brief discussion, or a way to divide the class into teams (based on student responses). They can be posted on the front board or written on a bulletin board. Students can be given the responsibility for providing the "quote of the day" or the "quotes of the week." Several art teachers I (Ellen) know post an art dilemma of the day, such as, "If a monkey is handed a brush and paints a picture, is it abstract art?"

Introduce variety. Plan for a "change of pace" activity. One example might be to assign each student a famous person to research and provide a biography of the person. Take turns letting the rest of the members of the class ask questions to find the identity of the person. Schedule brief reports throughout the month. Set up a round-robin or debate schedule. Use cooperative learning strategies. Have students give a brief talk on their lives as a student in your class and videotape their performances to play back for the class. Not only do students enjoy seeing themselves on tape, but the tape can be used periodically for review. Also, it provides feedback to students on their communication skills.

Integrate with other disciplines. English (or science, math, or physical education) does not have to stand alone as a separate entity. Bring in artwork associated with your subject. Play related music for the students. Or better yet, have your student musicians play for the class. Teach students dance steps, or invite a member of the community to do it for you. Coordinate your lessons with other members of your faculty. Many middle schools today are organized in teams, which will facilitate the planning process to work collaboratively. In non-teamed situations, you will need to seek out teachers from different areas who are interested in joining in collaborative efforts.

Incorporate carefully planned games. Prepare questions and answers in advance for a game of Jeopardy or Tic Tac Toe. Try baseball, where correct answers move a player around the diamond, or football, where correct answers advance a player 10 yards. If you have a behaviorally responsible class, you can even play volleyball with a nerf ball, where the right to serve is earned by correctly answering a question. A simulated

Pictionary game will serve to reinforce vocabulary words in German class or in a science class. Students can play as an entire class or in teams of four. The latter, of course, will be noisy, but as you circulate around the room, you will see that the level of involvement will be quite high. I (Ellen) have seen middle school and high school classes in which teachers have students create their own board games. There are also many commercially produced simulation games, many of which are now available on CDs, that are excellent in the classroom. Games are excellent ways to review material and reinforce knowledge.

Invite guest speakers and parents to your room to share their real-life experiences. Encourage students to find people who are especially interesting and can talk about how a particular subject relates to their lives. We have seen how classes become meaningful to students when they interact with a speaker. An insurance actuary even made probability theory seem interesting. A Vietnamese immigrant talked about how she viewed the English language. A homeless person told his story about losing control over his life. Bring the real world into your classroom so students can relate on a personal level.

Initiate correspondence. Arrange for a pen pal for your students, as a class or with individuals. This can be in your own school, with another school in your district, or a school in another part of the country or the world. Many students are successfully communicating with pen pals through e-mail. The Peace Corps will match a teacher with a Peace Corps volunteer through their program called World Wise Schools. They will also provide information on retired volunteers living in your area who are interested in getting involved with your students. Again, this strategy will help to personalize the school experience.

Use multiple resources. Bring in library books and CDs as well as videotapes. Pre-screen videotapes for relevant and appropriate content, and show only the sections that are meaningful. Arrange for students to have access to the Internet. Arrange for students to go on "virtual field trips," such as the Colonial Williamsburg Electronic Field Trip or the Tramline Volcano Field Trip. Contact museums to see if they have "traveling trunks" of artifacts that they will loan to public schools. Check with universities, too. Teacher education programs may have resources available to enliven your lessons. Having material available at different levels will help meet the varying ability levels of your students.

Include rewards. Build fun into your classroom every week, especially with activities that are seen as rewards for hard work. Students also react positively to prizes. Typically, teachers use candy, but there can be problems such as food allergies and candy wrappers on the floor, as well as sugar "highs" and "lows." Although giving prizes all the time can be costly and may lose meaning if done too frequently, bestowing awards of some type from time to time will get the students' attention. The gift can be an honor as well as a tangible item. Many teachers have effectively used tokens that they distribute and later collect for extra points or other rewards that their particular students find desirable.

Attitude and Values

Beginning teachers often get caught up in collecting specific techniques and exercises and supposedly foolproof lesson plans. You can't prevent boredom and conduct interesting classes simply by memorizing a series of activities that have worked for others.

As we say throughout this book, the specifics of what you do are not as important as your general attitude and basic values. If you believe that learning should be fun as well as hard work, that humor and play are important parts of school, then boredom can be kept at bay. The elements of surprise, laughter, spontaneity, variability, and high energy can be customized to fit your unique personality and teaching style. The key is to engage the learner by doing anything and everything you can think of.

If you develop solid relationships with your students, and create an open classroom environment, you will find that your mistakes and miscalculations will be forgiven. You don't have to pick the perfect activity or classroom lesson and expect it to work flawlessly every time. Sometimes, you will find that you have to try two, three, or even more different structures before you find something that really engages your students. The key factor is to give yourself permission to be playful and spontaneous and surprising. Learning need not be considered drudgery. If you expect your classroom to be spirited and interesting and exciting, then you can help make it so.

9

Eating Lunch

There are usually several choices in a school of where to eat lunch, and the decision is not merely one related to ingesting food. Lunch period is when a lot of informal networking goes on, when friends are made, when gossip and information are traded, when political alliances are formed, and even when mentoring takes place. It is a time to debrief and support one another. It is also about the only time during the hectic day in which you can talk to adults about what is going on in your life.

CHOICES, CHOICES

Although you could elect to use your lunch period to catch up on work or simply recover in solitude from the morning's stress, we strongly recommend that as a newcomer to the school community, you use all available opportunities to forge new relationships. For that reason, it might even be a good idea for you to experiment with as many different lunch settings as you can, making the rounds, so to speak, before you eventually settle on a routine place.

Your decision about where to eat lunch will depend on several factors: the cuisine available and whether it suits your taste and budget, whether the setting is a comfortable environment for you, and most important, who is in attendance and how they treat you. Some groups may virtually ignore you or even act somewhat put off that you are attempting to join a relatively intact culture. Other groups may be some-what cautious and suspicious, watching you carefully to see if you are "their kind of person" in terms of basic values and personality. Trust us, though, somewhere around the school are other individuals and groups that would be utterly delighted to have you join them. You just have to take the time to investigate what options are available.

The most obvious place to eat is in the teachers' dining room. This is usually adjacent to the school cafeteria. Often, there is a menu tailored to adult tastes. In some schools, most teachers gather there, whether they have brought lunches or not.

In newer schools, each department may have a workroom that attracts the faculty from that subject area. In other schools, there are various workrooms or lounges spaced throughout the building(s), where teachers gather.

At one school, I (Ellen) found a group of teachers who identified themselves as the "upstairs lunch bunch." This was a mixed group of people from different departments who met in a spacious workroom. Word of mouth brought people to the location, as it was a lively group. There were microwaves to use if you brought a lunch; otherwise, you could walk to the cafeteria to buy food and bring it upstairs. It was far from my classroom but worth the walk for the spirited conversa-tions that took place.

Most schools will have a group that likes to discuss politics. Others like to play games, like Trivial Pursuit. Some have televisions going for the news or soap operas.

As must be readily apparent, teachers group themselves together during lunch according to a number of variables: the geographic proximity of their rooms, their ages (older and younger), their political opinions or lifestyles, their teaching specialties, or their physical or social attractiveness, to mention just a few. You will find it fascinating research just to observe the various groups in action and try to figure out what binds them together.

Things also become complicated when you have multiple interests and roles in the school. If you coach a sport but do not teach physical education classes, you have to decide whether to eat with the coaches, your department, or a group of people you see as potential friends.

From time to time, you may enjoy eating lunch with the students. Visit the cafeteria. Sit down with a group. Or invite them to bring their lunches to your room. You'll have a chance to talk to them informally. Let them lead the conversation. Let them ask you questions. Learn about their worlds by listening rather than controlling the conversation. Sometimes, they might even forget you are a teacher, or even an adult, and a whole new world will open up before your eyes and ears in which you will really get a feeling for what it's like to be a teenager again.

THE CONSEQUENCES OF THE DECISION

Regardless of the place you choose, you will want to consider carefully the consequences of your decision. Some groups are notorious for the complaining and whining that goes on. It can be very depressing to hear adults berate the students and their parents day in and day out. Some people can be quite cynical about the state of education and the teaching profession. Each and every lunch period is spent taking turns complaining about how awful things are in the school, how unmotivated and unruly the kids are today, and how non-supportive the administration is. Then, particular staff members are selected as a focus for bash and gossip. Even if some of the complaints and criticisms are true, a new teacher does not need to be subjected to such negative energy in the middle of the day. Furthermore, such teachers will not want to have someone like you around who is upbeat and enthusiastic; their atmosphere thrives on pessimism.

In other lunch groups, strategic planning takes place. Science teachers plan a field trip. Two teachers plan an interdisciplinary unit: The American History teacher will begin a unit on the Great Depression when the junior English teacher assigns *The Grapes of Wrath* by John Steinbeck. Teachers brainstorm new ideas, share techniques that work, and take pride in their successes. They exchange ideas on classroom management and discipline or even compare notes about what works with some students who are particularly tough to handle. These are high-energy, motivated teachers who keep students' best interests in mind. Such teachers will welcome a new addition; their atmosphere thrives on optimism.

Some lunch groups develop a norm in which any school-related conversation is prohibited. These teachers prefer to talk instead about their personal lives, their families and friends, social and political events, books and movies, and/or community activities. Such individuals prefer to get away from school for a little while; they want to get to know one another, not as teachers but as human beings.

Every school will have its own options available, not only centered around larger groups but also smaller arrangements of two and three teachers who get together. As much as you will feel the attraction to settle down by yourself or with another new teacher you have befriended, force yourself to reach out to others. Even if you later decide you'd rather eat alone or with one friend, you will at least have circulated enough within the school to meet the faculty and staff and know what options are available.

FINAL ADVICE

Wherever you eat lunch, don't try to grade papers or take care of other paperwork. Many teachers unions worked very hard to get a "duty free" lunch, and you may be reproached by colleagues, some gently and some not so gently, if you bring papers to work on or even mail to read during lunch.

You must build into your day some structures that will keep you mentally alert and physically nourished. There are few jobs as exhausting as that of a high school teacher, and the lunch period provides a critical time for you to replenish your energy, both nutritionally and emotionally, before you once again jump back into the fray.

10

Connecting With Students

In spite of all the training you've had in teaching methods, technology, use of materials, and classroom management, it is through your relationships with students that you affect and influence them most dramatically. You only have to recall your own most important mentors and effective teachers to realize that it wasn't the stuff they knew that was so important, or how brilliant they were as lecturers, or how skilled they were in organizing their lessons; rather, it was who they were as human beings. Somehow, some way, they were able to connect with you so that you felt respected and cared for. You weren't just a student to them; you were someone who really mattered.

The connection you felt to your best teachers was built on trust and caring. These were people in your life who seemed to be able to reach you at a core level. They nourished not only your mind but also your heart and spirit. During times when you were most impressionable, perhaps even most vulnerable, these teachers were there for you. With them in your corner, you didn't feel so misunderstood, so confused, so alone.

BEING VISIBLE AND ACCESSIBLE

I've (Ellen) often wondered whether the most good I've done at school was in the hallways rather than in the classroom. It is during class changes that I made contact with as many students as I could, offering a few encouraging words or a smile. I tried to make myself as visible as I could in the school, so that kids would get used to seeing me visiting their worlds, rather than always staying in my own classroom. During my preparation period, I would visit the art room or the science room, for example. I wanted students to know that I really cared about them, and I did this by making myself as accessible as I could.

Many students spend more quality time with their teachers in any given day than they do with their own parents. With so many parents working—and some working more than one job—students today often seek out a teacher to talk to before or after school, when something is bothering them. You never know when a student will approach you with, "Can I talk to you for a minute?" It will usually be more than a minute, and you never know what the subject will be. The range of topics is extremely wide. Usually, it will be when no one else is around, which means at the end of the day when you are ready to go home. Here are just a few examples of the kinds of concerns students may bring to you:

- "I just found out I'm pregnant. What should I do?"
- "My dad took off, and we don't know when he's coming back. I'm not sure I even care."
- "I was thinking of dropping out of school. I really need to earn some more money."
- "I think I've got a drinking problem. I don't know. Probably not, but I've been blacking out lately."
- "My boyfriend wants to break up with me. Isn't there some way I can deal with this?"
- "There's this girl I like in your sixth hour class. How do you think I could approach her?"

- "I have no idea what college I should go to, or even if I should go to college at all."
- "I've been so depressed that lately, I've been thinking about . . . you know . . . maybe hurting myself."
- "I can't concentrate lately. On anything."

In each of these examples, students are connecting with you. They are reaching out to you. More than asking for advice or counseling, they are saying they trust you. You are one of the few adults in their lives whom they trust enough to confide their most pressing problems, their most confusing struggles. Whereas in so many other areas, being younger or less experienced than your colleagues is a distinct disadvantage, when it comes to connecting to students, you will find them far more willing to approach you because you are new. They will appreciate your greater enthusiasm and excitement. They will like the fact that you have no history with the school and so will appear safer. In many cases, you will also be closer to their age.

Your job is *not* to solve their problems, which you have little time for anyway. You cannot serve as their counselor, which you have little training for. Instead, you use your relationships with students to be a good listener, to support them, and to encourage them to make sound decisions. In some cases, your main job is to get the student some help and make an appropriate referral. But you will be amazed what you can do for kids simply by connecting with them, letting them know that you really care.

Listen, Don't Talk

In connecting with students, your primary role is as a listener, not a talker, and *especially* not an advice giver. In fact, in some instances, giving advice to kids is about the worst thing you can do. If things don't work out the way they hoped, they will blame you for the rest of their lives. Even worse, if the advice you offer *does* work out well, you have taught them to depend on you (or other adults) in the future. You have reinforced the idea that they don't know what's best for themselves, and they can't make their own decisions.

Rather than telling students what to do with their lives—and you certainly will have some rather strong opinions on the issues that concern them—you should instead concentrate on building a strong connection in which they feel heard and understood by you. There are certain skills used by counselors, called "active listening," that you may want to get some training in when you have the time. Essentially, these skills help you to communicate your interest and then reflect back what you've heard in such a way that the other person can work out the problem. Here are some tips for listening well to your students:

You must start with clearing your mind of all distractions. Take a deep breath to transition from what you were doing to being receptive to what the student has to say. Give the student your undivided attention. You may find this to be more difficult than it sounds, as you turn away from what you were doing and look directly at the student. Resist the temptation to look over the student's shoulder to see who is walking by your room. Your body language will reflect your concern and level of focus on the student. Likewise, observe the body language of the student. Is the student conveying messages that are consistent or inconsistent with what he or she is staying?

Listen without interrupting. If you have to ask a question (and often they are unnecessary), ask for clarification or elaboration. The best questions are "open" rather than "closed," meaning that they sound less interrogative and more expansive. Compare, for instance, the difference between the following conversations:

Student: "My friends just don't seem to get it. They keep pushing me and pushing me but don't take no for an answer."

Teacher: "Do they listen to you when you tell them you've had enough."

Student: "No."

Teacher: "Do you think they want you to just follow them blindly?"

Student: "I don't know."

In this series of "closed" questions, the teacher asks things that can be answered by single word responses, closing off deeper communication. This is quite different from the style exhibited in this alternative conversation:

Student: "My friends just don't seem to get it. They keep pushing me and pushing me but don't take no for an answer."

Teacher: "What has happened in the past when you try to tell them no?"

Student: "They just ignore me mostly. It's like they don't even care what I think. They only seem to want to be friends with me as long as I go along with them. But I'm not allowed to have my own opinions."

You can see from this elaboration that by asking a more open question, the exploration continues to include other areas of concern to the student, giving you more detailed information about their problem.

We are not saying, by the way, that you should even ask such questions in the limited time you have. But if you must ask questions, phrase them in such a way that they do not elicit one-word answers. This means generally asking "What?" or "How?" rather than "Do you . . . ?"

And now, a brief "time out" for a quiz:

Why should you not ask "why" questions?

Your answer: "I don't know."

That's correct. Most of the time you ask someone "Why?", especially a kid, they will respond with "I don't know."

"Why do you do drugs?"

Student shrugs.

"Why do you keep throwing your homework away when you know it's going to get you in trouble?"

"I don't know."

"Why do you keep saying you don't know?"

"I don't know."

You get the point.

Summarize what you understand. The best way to let students know that they have been heard and understood is *not* to say, "I understand." This is not only a simplistic a response but unlikely to be believed. The best way to show that you have listened carefully to someone, and understood not only the surface message but the deeper feelings and thoughts they are expressing, is to reflect back what you have heard. This takes considerable training and practice, but at its basic level, it goes something like this:

Student: "I'm not sure I understand this assignment."

Teacher: "I can see that you are a little confused."

Student: "Yeah. I mean, I thought on the last test that I understood things pretty good, but I didn't do so well."

Teacher: "You're feeling disappointed and a little discouraged. You want to do much better on this one."

Student: "I've been thinking lately that maybe this just isn't my thing. Maybe I'm not cut out for this subject. I mean, I like it and all, but . . ."

Teacher: "You're saying that although you really like what we are doing, it's hard for you, more challenging than you thought. You're wondering if maybe you should try something else."

Student: "Don't get me wrong. I like you and all. And I like this class a lot. It's just . . . I don't know." (Shrugs)

Teacher: "You don't really want to give up, but I hear you asking for more help and support."

From this brief conversation, you can see how carefully this teacher is listening. She is not asking questions (not one!) but simply listening and observing the student, decoding the messages that are being communicated, and reflecting back what she understands. The beauty of this sort of approach is that even if your reflections are not accurate, the student will correct the inaccuracy, and this, too, leads to deeper exploration:

Student: "Well, I would like some more support and all. It's just . . ."

Teacher: "You're feeling uneasy asking for help like this because you prefer to work things out on your own."

Student: "No, that's not it at all. I don't mind asking for help. It's just that I don't want to bother you."

It is beyond the scope of this chapter or book to teach you all (or even most) of what you need to get started in connecting with your students in this way. But there are other resources available (see our book, *Counseling Skills for Teachers* [2000]) that can introduce you to these methods, as well as courses and workshops you might attend at a later time. For now, we just want you to understand that connecting with students is not just about your best intentions but also your skills, and these you can develop a lot further.

Your ongoing relationships with students, rather than any specific guidance you offer, will make the greatest difference. You don't have the time or the training to do any real counseling—besides, there are professionals in your school who have been specifically trained for that work. But within short periods of time, you can help your students feel supported and understood. At times, you can even encourage them to work toward small, realistic, incremental goals that are in the directions they would like to go. More than anything else, however, just try to make strong connections. You will be amazed how healing a supportive relationship can be. Many students just need attention and to know someone is paying attention to them and cares about them.

REACH OUT TO STUDENTS

One way you personalize your subject area to your students' lives is to continuously make connections to what matters most to them. Use examples related to sports, contemporary music, or current events. Better yet, ask students to articulate ways that what you're doing relates to their lives.

Outside of your class, make a point to visit students where they hang out. Attend athletic competitions. Go to school plays and concerts. Volunteer to be a chaperon at school dances, or judge a debate.

Teachers frequently call students' homes to talk to parents. One secret is to call home just to talk to the student. The conversation is private. The other students don't see or hear you targeting a classmate for a conversation, to reprimand, or to praise, any of which can be equally embarrassing to the student in front of his peers. This is particularly effective for students whom you sense are needy for attention.

I (Ellen) have done this unintentionally—trying to reach a parent for help regarding uncooperative behavior, for example, and ending up talking to the student when the parent wasn't home. I told him I was calling regarding his behavior and asked him to relay a message to his parents. I found my mission was accomplished when his behavior improved after the phone call. I did not have to speak to his parents—just discussing his behavior privately over the telephone served as a stimulus for him to change it.

You can also make a point to call students at home, not just when they are in trouble but when they've done something you especially appreciate. Tell students when you are proud of them, when you've seen some improvement in their work, or when you've noticed some extra effort extended.

In addition to making phone calls, you can also write notes to students. In such brief communications, you can give them encouragement and support, make suggestions for books or articles you think they might like, or even take the time to say some things privately that might be helpful for them to hear.

SOME QUICK INTERVENTIONS

If you have taken the time to develop solid relationships with your students, then it is far more likely they will be open to necessary interventions you must employ.

One time, I (Ellen) turned around to see Howard with his arms around a girl from behind, trying to reach his pencil. Howard was a playful young teenager who liked to get attention from the girls. This time, however, his behavior could have been interpreted as sexual harassment. When I called him to my desk, he quickly broke his hold on the girl and came to talk to me. I very privately and quietly brought to his attention that this behavior could be misinterpreted. I tried to tell him this in a way that was less a censure than a good-natured "word to the wise." He was open to this feedback because he trusted me and knew I wasn't putting him down; I was really trying to help him avoid an unpleasant situation. He was very careful of his behavior after that exchange.

This interaction could easily have turned out differently. Some students will take offense or feel threatened by invasions of their privacy. You can extend yourself to students and reach out to them, but ultimately, they will let you know if and when they are ready to respond to your overtures.

THINGS TO CONSIDER
WHEN CONNECTING WITH STUDENTS

- Listen carefully without interrupting.
- Listen not only for what the student is saying, but also for what is being implied beneath the surface.
- Stay neutral and don't judge the student, or trust may be breached.
- Communicate with your body, face, eyes, your whole being, that you are intensely interested in what students are saying.
- Show compassion and empathy in your manner and style.
- Whenever possible, don't let yourself be interrupted or distracted when a student is confiding in you.
- Prove that you've understood what was said by occasionally responding with reflections of feeling and content that you heard.
- Avoid giving advice or telling students what to do with their lives.
- Make yourself as visible and accessible as you can.
- If you must ask questions, don't interrogate kids; instead, ask open-ended inquiries that encourage them to elaborate.
- Look carefully for signs of severe distress; if a student does seem to be in danger of harm or abuse, you must report it to the administration.
- At the end of a conversation, summarize what you heard, and ask the student to summarize what he/she has said.
- Make appropriate referrals to the school counselor or other professionals when a student could profit from such help. Secure a commitment from the student to do something about his or her situation to get additional help. If convenient, you can offer to go with the student to introduce him or her to the professional.
- Follow up on the conversations by remembering to ask students how they're doing and what they've done about the problem since you last talked.

CONNECTING WITH DIFFICULT STUDENTS

In spite of your best intentions, there will be a number of students who don't respond to your noble overtures. Don't let them get you down. As a beginning teacher, you are often assigned to some of the most challenging groups of kids, those who are unmotivated or who may be somewhat difficult to handle.

Although all teachers wouldn't necessarily share the same definition of who a difficult student is, there is some consensus as to which ones may challenge you the most in your efforts to reach them:

- The angry student looks sullen, with a chip on his shoulder. No matter what you do, he will resist your efforts.
- The withdrawn student is certainly not a behavior problem; quite the opposite, she may sit passively in the back of the room or even sleep with her head on the desk, completely unengaged in the lesson.
- The quiet student just doesn't talk at all. He may or may not be paying attention; you really can't tell. No matter what you do to try and draw him out, he is so shy that he just smiles enigmatically.
- The student who is in over her head feels like she is so far behind, there is no point in even trying to cooperate in your class. She has given up all hope.
- The procrastinator continually plays games with you. He always has excuses for why he doesn't have his work completed. He may be wickedly charming, but he manages to avoid doing much that is useful.
- The addicted student is strung out on drugs or alcohol. Her attention is, at best, fleeting. She sits in the back of the room with a glassy-eyed stare.
- The overly social student is always flirting or disturbing others around him. You stop him a dozen times, but he doesn't seem to respond to the corrections.
- The class clown may be motivated by either the need to express her sense of humor or something more perverse.

Regardless of his intentions, he is constantly the center of attention, drawing the other students' focus away from what you're trying to teach.

We could go on *a lot* longer with our list. In fact, competitions among teachers as to who has the most annoying, disruptive, difficult students are a frequent topic of conversation in some lunch groups. We don't mean to frighten you with the idea that you will encounter so many kids who are uncooperative and difficult to deal with. We just want you to be realistic in your expectations of what you can do with the time, resources, and training that is available to you. Then, there are the family, peer, and neighborhood environments to which these students return after they leave school, environments whose influence is out of your control. Chapter 12 explores further the issue of dealing with difficult students.

You may not be able to help everyone in your classes. You probably won't make a significant difference in the lives of most of your students. However, there will likely be some who will thank you immediately. Others will return years later to tell you what a difference you made when you were not even aware of it. But in every class, there will be a few who will be profoundly influenced by what you do and who you are. That is what will sustain you.

11

Communicating With Parents

Silence. That was what I (Ellen) heard on the other end of the telephone. Complete stillness except for soft breathing. I had just called a parent to say what a pleasure it was to have her child in my class, how attentive she was, and what good grades she was getting.

"Yes," the parent responded expectantly, "and what's your point?"

"That's all," I replied, a bit confused. Here I was telling her what a pleasure her daughter was to work with, how attentive she was in class, that she turned her homework in on time, was making steady progress, and the mother seemed almost defensive.

"Oh," she finally said. "I was waiting for the bad news." She laughed, then said, as if to confirm there was no other reason for the call, "Are you sure?"

"Yes, I'm sure," I said, not at all sure if the mother believed me yet. "I hope she continues to do well in the future."

AUTHORS' NOTE: Throughout this chapter, we use the term "parents" to mean parents or guardians.

117

"Well," the parent said with relief. "Thank you so much for calling! It's so nice to have a teacher call with a good report. You just made my day! I appreciate your taking the time to call."

As I hung up the phone, I'm sure we both had smiles on our faces.

Parents enjoy hearing about their children's positive experiences, both academic and social. They don't get to see how a child interacts with, and responds to, the variety of people and experiences in the school environment. Much of what they hear is filtered through the often limited reports from the children: "How was school today?" the parent asks. "Fine. What's there to eat?" You provide parents with a "window" into their child's world. In ideal circumstances, your conversations with parents about their children should include a balance of both supportive as well as constructive reports.

THE IMPORTANCE OF PARENT INVOLVEMENT

It's extremely important to establish communication with parents/guardians early in the year and maintain it until the end.

The National Parent Teacher Association (PTA) reports from their research that when parents are involved in their child's education, the child does better academically, regardless of the socioeconomic status or ethnic/cultural background of the family, and regardless of the age of the child. Not only that, but there is increased likelihood of the child displaying cooperative behavior, positive attitudes, and completing and submitting homework on time. With parental involvement, students are more likely to have regular attendance, to graduate, and to go on to some form of post-secondary education.

The National PTA has six National Standards for Parent/Family Involvement Programs. The topics include: (1) improving communication between parents and schools,

(2) providing programs to improve parenting skills, (3) increasing parent involvement in student learning, (4) providing more opportunities for parent volunteering, (5) increasing participation of parents in school decision making and advocacy, and (6) closer collaboration between teachers and other community organizations. We will take a look at how to develop the initial rapport with parents.

BUILDING PARENT RELATIONSHIPS

At the beginning of each semester, most schools now require that the teacher send home a course syllabus or class expectancy sheet. At the bottom of the page, you can include a place for the parent or guardian to sign, indicating that he or she has read the paper and is aware of the objectives, grading policy, and content of the class.

The written communication does not have to stop there. You can send a more personal letter home, introducing yourself to the parents at the beginning of the school year. Share a little bit about your background, your interests, your educational philosophy, what the course will entail for the students, and how parents can help. Periodically, or on a regular basis, you can send a general note home informing the parents of class activities, upcoming field trips, events or projects, or asking for volunteer time or the donation of objects that would be useful in the classroom. Email can also be a useful way to communicate with parents to solicit their input as well as to provide reports of student progress.

Many parents will welcome the opportunity to be involved. Some have other commitments and are only available on a short-term basis. These parents might chaperone a field trip. Or they will bake for a special occasion if it is permitted. They will donate products or supplies from home. They would be willing to visit the class to be part of an audience for a performance or judge a presentation. Many have an area of expertise they would be happy to share. They just need to be informed of what is needed, when, and where. Some will be available on a regular basis; others, not at all, due to family and work schedules. Even if they cannot be included or involved, they will benefit from the information you provide about what is happening during the school day in the student's classes—not only for their own knowledge but as tools to begin conversations with their children.

Within an aboriginal community in Australia, one school principal decided to reshape the whole concept of a school to be more culturally relevant and responsive to parents. He gathered together as many parents as he could, calling and visiting the others who could not make it to the scheduled meetings. In his presentation, he made it clear that the school was an extension of their homes. As such, they were invited to visit as often as they like, just as they would drop in to see neighbors and friends. Although this might seem a bit chaotic and inappropriate in many North American settings, the whole idea of this plan was to make parents more active partners in the educational process.

I (Jeffrey) have noticed a similar pattern in other indigenous cultures in which I have worked. While preparing primarily native Hawaiian teachers in some of the outer islands, it was very common for their families to visit at any time throughout the day. The students' parents would come and bring food to share, often sitting in on the classes so they could see what was going on. The students themselves would bring their own infant or preschool children, and everyone in the class would take turns caring for the children.

These two examples illustrate the breaking down of traditional boundaries between school and home, in order to work more collaboratively and cooperatively with families. You can take a huge step in this direction simply by letting parents know that you value their input and contributions.

Another way to build rapport with parents is to attend the programs when they come to watch their children, whether on the ball field, in the theater, or at an academic competition. Yet another option is to invite families to come before or after school, or in the evening to view a "gallery" or "museum" of student work. With this invitation, you not only display students' work and give recognition for their accomplishments, but also provide a venue for parents to interact with you in a more informal way. Hopefully, using the above suggestions, you will meet and get to know the parents in person before graduation day.

CONTACTING PARENTS

Schools send out grades on a regular basis and most, if not all schools also send out notices midway through the card-marking period to alert parents if their children are displaying socially unacceptable behavior and/or are making unsatisfactory progress (sometimes called "unsats") or are failing one or more classes. Parents are generally made aware of the mailing dates of these notices. Most schools have a form you can use at any time to send the information home.

Although we wish that all contacts home involved reporting good news—whether by telephone, email, or mailing a letter/postcard home—it is far more likely that we contact parents/guardians by phone because their child is being noncompliant or difficult socially, academically, or both.

When you are making such contacts, be as sensitive and noncritical as possible so that parents don't become unduly threatened and uncooperative themselves (obviously, they will not be thrilled to hear negative reports about their child). Emphasize that you share values with the parent regarding the student's welfare. Acknowledge, if appropriate, that this can be a difficult time between parents and children. Try to stay neutral, calm, and supportive.

If you are verbally attacked, or it is obvious the parent isn't listening, then disengage as best you can without making matters worse. Schedule a parent conference with the principal or another administrator present, or refer the parent to the counselor, dean, or assistant principal.

Basically, in these reports to parents, you are simply informing them of what you have observed. Provide specific examples of what has occurred. Mention a few of the student's strengths as well as weaknesses. Then, ask for the parents' help with *your* problem (and it really is your concern).

One such conversation might begin like this: "Hello Mrs. Tran. I am calling to talk to you about your daughter. As you know, she is a young woman who is very spirited, enthusiastic, and energetic. She is a lot of fun to be around and I can count on her to help enliven class when things become a little dull." (This is a diplomatic way of saying that she has attention deficit problems, is sometimes disruptive and unruly, and is difficult to control. Of course, Mrs. Tran will already know this.)

"I do have some challenges, however, helping her to stay on task as she has a lot of different interests." (She is all over the place and does not concentrate well or stay focused for long). "For instance, the other day, everyone was working quietly on an assignment and Tina kept throwing paper clips at a few of her friends across the aisle—I'm sure you are aware that she has quite a few friends." (Again, the behavior problems are framed within a more balanced, positive context).

"I was wondering if we might put our heads together and figure out some ways that we could help Tina to improve her concentration, and at the same time, to improve her schoolwork, which is nowhere near her potential. I think we both agree that she is a bright girl who, with a little guidance, could improve significantly." (With the conversation set up in this way, Mrs. Tran is more than willing to be helpful. She also does not feel a "loss of face.")

Teachers often call home when there is trouble brewing. The student is being a pest in class, or is not turning in work, or might even be failing. The parents of many students have even become conditioned over time to associate bad news with teacher calls home, and they may have become understandably defensive. It is as if we are criticizing their parental competence, as if we're saying their kids have turned out the way they have because the parents don't know what they're doing.

Actually, we do think that, on occasion. Many of the students we see come from homes with very unhealthy living situations: poverty, unemployment, physical or sexual abuse, neglect, excessive alcohol consumption, drug abuse, little supervision, little help with homework, angry, even violent behavior among the adults, inconsistent or minimal discipline, and absolutely no support for excellence in school. Students in such situations experience hopelessness and despair and a lack of positive role models. No wonder some students struggle so much.

Still, parents are the keys to any lasting change efforts we might wish to promote. They can be our best friends or our worst enemies. If they are unsupportive, they can easily sabotage any potential their children have to succeed in school or in life. Often, what we are doing seems threatening to them, or at least incomprehensible. Even if their kids wanted to do their homework or prepare for class, they may be teased or scorned mercilessly by their siblings, parents, and friends. That is why it is so crucial that we connect not only with our students but also their parents, in order to build positive relationships.

One easy way for you to begin is to find a reason, almost *any* reason, to call parents, email them, or write them a note when their children do something that is positive, or at least a step in the right direction. Here are some examples of positive calls home you might make:

- "I've been really impressed that your daughter has come to class on time 3 days in a row. I just wanted to let you know that whatever you're doing, it seems to be working."
- "Your son turned in a paper to me this week, and although he definitely needs work with his punctuation and grammar, the ideas he expressed were really interesting. I just wanted to let you know that I think he's got some real potential."

- "I just finished grading the latest exam. Although the total score your daughter got wasn't nearly as high as I think she is capable of doing, I really liked some of her creative responses. She really has a wonderful imagination."
- "I wanted to let you know that your son really helped me out today. There was a fight that broke out in class, and he helped me regain order by acting quickly to break things up. He shows some real leadership at times. I'd love to try and build on that."
- "As you know, sometimes your daughter can be a bit challenging to keep under control. I really find her a joy to have in class, though. Her sense of humor and playfulness are lovely. I'm working with her now to be a bit more restrained at times in her comments, and I think she's making fine progress. I just wanted you to know that."

Okay, some of these are a stretch. But you get the general idea. Look for the slightest signs of improvement in your students, any evidence at all that they are growing, learning, or changing, and reinforce that behavior directly by telling them how much you appreciate their efforts. Also make a point to tell their parents. Keep the communication ongoing.

It's a good idea to keep a record of your contacts home, whether you spoke with parents or the student. Note the date, time, and nature of the conversation. Also, if you agreed to do anything that requires action of some kind, make a note in your planner to follow up, and then do so.

OPEN HOUSE

Most schools hold an Open House or Back to School Night for parents to meet the teachers. The Open House typically takes one of two formats. The most common is one in which the parents are given a copy of the school schedule, and each class meets for an abbreviated period, maybe 10 minutes. During this time, teachers introduce themselves, describe the content of the class, review the grading policy, and perhaps show examples of student work. It's worth your while to spend a little time on making your room attractive for this event.

Usually, there are a few minutes for general questions. Sometimes parents will ask questions or make suggestions to which you are not prepared to respond. A gracious way to handle such a situation is to thank them for bringing the idea to your attention, and go on. There is no time given for individual attention or conversation regarding a specific student during this format; therefore, a private conference can be suggested for a later date.

Other helpful hints include the following:

- Prepare a PowerPoint presentation to support the main points of your introduction. Parents will see firsthand how technology is being integrated into their child's education.
- Inform your audience as to how they can get in touch with you and when they might expect a response—during your prep period, before school, after school, or in the evening. Make sure to let parents know how they can make arrangements to have a conference with you.
- Distribute a handout with pertinent information or a copy of your syllabus, because the time goes so quickly, and sometimes parents forget what they hear. Also, it will keep you "on task." And if you get nervous easily, handouts are a good idea because parents will likely look at the sheet of paper rather than at you.
- Practice what you are going to say aloud for timing—ten minutes will be long for some of you, but will go by quickly for others.
- Pass around a "sign-in sheet" that indicates student's name and parent(s)/guardian(s) names. (Remember, the last names can be different.)

The second format is where teachers sit in their rooms, or together in one room, such as the cafeteria, library/media center, and/or gymnasium, and the parents line up to speak to each of their children's teachers. In this scenario, teachers introduce themselves and then give a brief description of the course and a quick report on the child's progress. Although more personal in nature than the first format, there still isn't time to go into any problems in depth. A private, individual conference can be suggested for a later date.

FACE-TO-FACE CONTACTS

Formal or informal parent conferences are other fruitful methods of communication. Such meetings can include a single parent or a whole group of people, including the student, his or her parents, other family members, school administrators, a counselor, and others (psychologist, social worker, special education teacher) who might be relevant. Including students will give them the opportunity to express their own feelings and perspectives on behavior and academic achievement. Some schools utilize student-led conferences, where the student is responsible for planning and leading.

It is important to be prepared for the conference. First, consider setting the stage. If the conference is to be held in your room, you may need to rearrange the furniture so there will be comfortable places for the parents and you to sit face to face. If you sit behind your desk, you create a symbolic barrier; sitting across a table or in front of one another is a friendlier approach. Try to find a time and place where you will not be disturbed. Post a note on your door indicating that a conference is in progress.

Create a folder for the conference in which to put assignments and examples of the student's work. You might also want to add your written descriptions of the student's behavior. Include a printout of the student's attendance record and grades as well.

The first impression you make is *very* important. Greet the parent(s) or guardian(s) as they enter the room. Introduce yourself, if this is the first meeting. Be sure to make eye contact with the adults, and say hello to the student if he or she is present. Use their names. As you guide the participants into the room, say something positive about the student. Let the parents look around the room. Talk about the class in general.

As you begin the conference, ask an open-ended question such as, "What does Lisi say about the class when she is at home?" See if you can gather information this way. Use your listening skills and watch the body language. Then, review the purpose of the conference—was it initiated by the parent? By you? Or, is this a regularly scheduled conference to review progress? If the student is present, have him or her state his or her view of the situation and his or her feelings about it.

Review the objectives for the class, and see if there are any problems. If so, identify strategies that might help resolve the problems. Be specific as you determine the child's responsibilities, the parents' or guardians' responsibilities, and your own role. Try to set a time line for what needs to be done, when, where, and how. The last step is to identify how progress will be evaluated and monitored.

In concluding the conference, thank the parents for coming, and invite each person to summarize his or her understanding of the conversation. Make plans for further communication with the adults, by telephone, letter, fax, email, another scheduled conference, or a progress report sent by the school.

After the conference, you can take time to write down some notes (if you didn't do so during the meeting). Reflect on what transpired, asking yourself the following questions:

- Did I give each of the participants time to share his or her views?
- Did I mention positive aspects of the student's behavior and work as well as the problem areas?
- Was I prepared with samples of the student's work and examples of behavior?
- Did I keep the focus on the student and not the school or the parent?

- Did I maintain my composure throughout the meeting, staying empathic and responsive?
- Was a specific plan developed to foster progress in the future?
- What was forgotten or neglected that I may wish to deal with in the future?

Making "house calls" is one other option to consider. Although time consuming, and perhaps risky without supervision and proper training, informal visits to a student's home with the parents' prior approval is another way that you can show how much you care. You can gain valuable information in that setting that would be inaccessible any other way.

ONGOING CONTACT

You can direct students to take home their graded or evaluated work with a note to have signed and returned as a way to make sure the parent is kept abreast of the student's progress. If you do this, make sure that each student returns the work with the appropriate signature. Those who don't return papers or projects need to have their parents contacted with respect to the grade or evaluation received *and* the fact that the student did not return the work as directed. (Check for validity of parent signatures, too.)

The school newsletter is another way to communicate with parents. By submitting articles that you or one of your students have written, you can let parents know what is going on in your classroom or with your club or team. You can also include photographs, which will make the article more attractive. Or, create your own teacher or class newsletter, on your own or with the help of your students. Software programs, such as Publisher, have made this an easy project.

Many schools have provided teachers with telephones and voice mail. Not only does this facilitate communication with parents, but also enables teachers to record outgoing messages that include daily overviews, activities, assignments, and reminders for parents and students.

Email and the Internet are increasingly facilitating communication with parents. It is a quick way to check on attendance, progress with assignments, and send reminders. Given passwords, individuals can check grades online.

Taking pictures of the students in various activities and sending them home is a fun way to let the parents know what the children are doing and what their involvement is. Another idea would be to make a videotape and take turns sending it home with each of the students. This would be an especially useful plan for students whose parents don't speak English.

Many teachers are creating their own Web sites and posting information online. If students and parents have access, this is a great tool to improve communication. You can let parents and students know when tests will be given and when homework and projects are due. You can post makeup assignments, class notes, rubrics for projects, references, and additional references and supplementary material to support parents as they help children prepare for their classes. If parents do not have computer access, you can send these items home on hard copy.

UNDERSTANDING LIMITED RESPONSES FROM PARENTS

There are many reasons why some parents make limited or no response to our efforts. For some, the problem is economic—work schedules prevent parents from calling or coming to the school. Many parents have limited access to a telephone during the work day, and even if they do have access, their calls will not be private, so they are unlikely to contact the school. Some parents have small children or elderly parents for whom they must care, or lack transportation and therefore are unable to come to school.

As you are aware, many parents have difficulties speaking English, or lack confidence in their language proficiency. This may also account for why they do not provide homework support. There may be cultural factors as well. In some cultures, education is left entirely to the teachers, for whom parents have great respect. These parents do not believe in crossing into the teacher's domain. Some parents have had negative experiences in the past and have chosen to avoid contact if at all possible.

While it can be frustrating and disappointing when our efforts do not bring the successes we would like, we hope you will be understanding and continue to work to encourage parent and family involvement. Many schools and districts are working to implement programs to improve parental involvement.

RECRUITING PARENTS AS ALLIES

We have frequently heard in staff lounges teachers complaining about parents as if they are the enemy, constantly undermining their efforts and blaming them when things go wrong. While a small minority of parents will be certainly unappreciative, uncooperative, or critical, most of them will be absolutely delighted that you care enough to communicate with them and solicit their help.

12

Dealing With Difficult Students

Beginning teachers are likely to be tested and challenged by students—a lot. This isn't personal; rather, it's a rite of passage. Teenagers often just test the limits of their behavior to see how far they can go, which actions will be tolerated, and which ones won't.

The good news is that your colleagues and administration know this, and they will give you some time to find your stride. You are likely to be reassured again and again by the dean, principal, and department head that this is normal behavior on the part of your students, and if you experience any predicaments with students you can't handle, you should refer them immediately for disciplinary action.

Most often, this means a student who

- Is consistently late to class
- Repeatedly does not bring in necessary supplies
- Threatens or disrespects you, publicly or privately
- Threatens or assaults another student

- Refuses to follow your instructions
- Disrupts the class with inappropriate behavior

Depending on the policies of your administration and the norms of your school, any or all of these behaviors will not be tolerated. Especially as a beginning teacher, you must expect (and request) support from other school personnel to help you keep your classes under control and your students' behavior within reasonable limits. It is simply not realistic for you to expect that you can handle all discipline problems yourself, even if you had the time to do so. At the same time, you must take responsibility by setting clear rules for behavior and implementing them consistently.

CLASSROOM MANAGEMENT

You have probably already had some preparation in the theory and methods of classroom management. This includes such areas as setting expectations for behavior, controlling the flow of activity, handling discipline problems, and keeping students engaged and motivated to learn. We will review some of these major concepts and urge you to keep them in mind *when*—not if—you encounter challenges with difficult students.

Prevention. By creating a comfortable environment and establishing rapport with your students, you set the stage for peaceful, cooperative classes. You will also need to establish rules and enforce them consistently. Routines will help your classroom to function smoothly. Welcoming your students to the room each day will give you an opportunity to interact with them as they enter. Plan for a smooth transition from one activity to the next.

Using highly motivational activities for instruction is another prevention tool. When you immediately capture student interest and make the topic relevant, you will gain their attention at the beginning of the period and they will have little time to act out.

You should also note (and perhaps recall from your own experiences as a student) that most kids are not particularly interested in what is offered in school, as they do not find it relevant to their most cherished interests (finding love, acceptance, approval, money, respect). They are forced to learn things that they would never select for themselves. They are subjected to routines and procedures that are, at best boring, and at worst, quite annoying. No wonder some students act out and become difficult to handle. In a sense, they are honestly communicating what they feel, which is boredom, anger, and frustration. Of course, your job is to engage students while helping them stay within appropriate boundaries. Therein lies the conflict.

GUIDELINES FOR ENGAGING STUDENTS

- Greet students at the door.
- State the objective. Students need to know what they will be expected to know and be able to do.
- Relate content to prior knowledge. Make sure students have the prerequisite knowledge and skills in order to meaningfully relate to your lesson.
- Plan for student involvement. At some point during the period, have students work with a partner or in a small group, to get them more actively engaged in their learning.
- Address learning styles and multiple intelligences. By integrating different learning styles, you offer a variety of activities to suit all different types of learners.
- Chunk material into manageable sections. Students will be successful if presented with small amounts of material, or sequences to a skill. This way they will see progress and not feel as overwhelmed.
- Focus on higher order thinking skills. Move away from facts and details. Plan for challenging engagement.
- Allow student input in decision making. When students have ownership in how they will process

material, they are more likely to follow through. Give them as much choice and control over their learning as possible.

- Organize activities that are relevant to real life. Students need connections to their world.
- Use concrete examples. Again, this will help students to relate to the subject you are presenting. Realia (real objects) and visual aids are extremely valuable.
- Elaborate on text material, if appropriate, and model reading strategies. Students need help developing their reading skills.
- Vary strategies. By changing formats of presentation and assessments from time to time, you will keep the students stimulated.
- Provide for movement. Students get tired sitting at a desk or table all day long (especially kinesthetic learners). They need to move around.
- Project enthusiasm. Your passion in itself can be motivating.
- Give prompt feedback. Giving feedback to students on their work—whether it is a response in class, comments on a new skill they've learned, or feedback on a homework assignment, an essay/report, or a test— is also highly motivating.
- Give lots of praise when it is deserved. Students benefit when it is confirmed that they have done well and are making progress, whether they're learning to type, throw a basketball, speak a new language, or learn a principle of physics.
- Keep your sense of humor and remember that students want to have fun.

Mild Intervention. There will be times when students lose interest and begin to daydream or engage in another activity. Minor discipline problems are to be expected. After all, you are working with adolescents. If this behavior does not interrupt the class, such as when a student is simply looking out the window, there are several ways you can respond. If it is not serious and will probably go away in a minute or two, consider the following options:

- Ignore undesired behavior. If it isn't bothering the other students and won't distract you, wait and see what happens.
- Use nonverbal communication. Use body language, such as pointing to the task.
- Stand near the student. Sometimes just moving closer to the student will be enough of an intervention to get the student to refocus attention to the assigned task.
- Give a verbal response. Gently, speak to the student to gain attention and draw the individual to the task.
- Use an "I" message. Tell the student how you feel when he or she is not paying attention.
- Make a direct appeal. Ask the student to refocus on the lesson.
- Remind student of rule(s) and expectations for the class.
- Try using humor to deal with the situation. Speak in a way that students will enjoy, and it may bring the distracted individual back to the task at hand.

If you find several students are disengaged, take this opportunity to evaluate what is going on in the classroom. Is there a message being sent to you? Is the activity paced too slowly? Too quickly? Are students confused? Is it too easy? Too difficult? Have you misjudged their attention spans? Maybe they are indicating that a change is needed. Treat such incidents as useful feedback in which the students are telling you that what you are doing is not working and it is time to try something else.

Major Interventions. When discipline becomes an issue, you will have to become more active and direct in your responses. You will need to quickly communicate with the student. Also, you may need to involve other people outside the classroom. Possible actions include the following:

- Request that the student put away whatever object currently has gained attention.
- Remove stimulus. Take the object away or call for security to take care of the situation.
- Encourage involvement. Ask the student to do something that would be attractive or intriguing to him or her. Give the student responsibility for something in the classroom.
- Give logical consequence. Remind the student of what action will follow if the behavior continues.
- Withdraw privilege. Let the student know there will be a change in the future, if compliance with the class rules does not take place.
- Change seat. Have the student sit in another location.
- Write a note to the student. In private, communicate your response to the unwanted/undesired behavior. You may be able to do this during class, if you are discreet.
- Contact parent or guardian. Call home and discuss the behavior.
- Give a detention. Have student stay after school.
- Send the student to the dean's office. As a last resort, direct the student to leave the class and report to the administrator responsible for discipline.

STUDENTS WITH ATTENTION DEFICITS

Among those difficult students most often mentioned by beginning and experienced teachers alike are those who have trouble staying focused. Students who have trouble concentrating, whether formally or informally diagnosed with attention deficit disorders such as ADHD (Attention Deficit Hyperactivity Disorder), can be challenging for both the teacher and the other students in the room. I (Ellen) remember one student in particular who always seemed to be the center of my attention—talking to other students, shouting out answers to questions, even walking around the room. The students in the class had difficulty with his constant interruptions as well, sometimes even expressing their frustrations aloud.

The following suggestions have been effective for handling students with attention deficits:

- Seat student near you. Your physical presence will help the student to focus on what is required.
- Provide for opportunities to change tasks.
- Prioritize "misbehaviors." Address the ones that you would most like to change first.
- Give reminders as students begin an unacceptable behavior. For example, speak to the individual who begins to get out of the assigned seat.
- Help students to self-monitor their behavior.
- Decrease distractions. You may need to put away artifacts and objects that you have collected and put on display. Even bulletin boards need to be assessed for their "busy-ness."
- Respond to repetitive questions with one-line answers. Acknowledge the student as briefly as possible and move on.
- Remind students that accuracy is as important as speed. Encourage students to spend extra time to make sure answers or responses are correct.
- Comment when desirable traits are displayed. Make sure the student gets positive feedback during the period.
- Give handshakes. Physical contact can be helpful.
- Be calm and clear. Remain composed.
- Assign classroom responsibilities. Provide for movement in the room.
- Confer with others. Work in collaboration with other teachers to develop a management plan to effectively work with attention deficit kids.

AVOID DIRECT CONFRONTATION

Whether with disengaged students, or those who are acting out dramatically, it should be considered a last resort to send the person out of the room. There are consequences to taking formal disciplinary action. For one thing, it brings attention to the fact that there was a problem you couldn't handle yourself. Although you are allowed a certain latitude in this regard, you don't want to resort to sending kids out of your classroom very frequently, or it may look like you haven't established control over your classes.

In general, whenever a student appears noncompliant, uncooperative, or defiant, whatever you do, you don't want to escalate matters by making a public show of authority or force—unless it is absolutely necessary. It is far better to censure privately. Speak in a low, calm voice. Give directions firmly but avoid threats.

Consider not touching students when there is a discipline problem. Some children will react violently—not only will they shake off the gesture, but they may attempt to strike back.

Remember: Everyone else in the room is watching closely to see how you handle yourself. There is a show going on, and you are the main attraction. You are being tested. Your response is crucial.

Remain cool, poised, and in control of yourself. Do not become defensive. Likewise, try not to put the student in a position in which he or she loses face in front of peers. This is a tough challenge but can be accomplished if you have established a reasonable discipline policy in the first place.

IMPLEMENTING A DISCIPLINE POLICY

Most schools have a formal discipline procedure that you are mandated to follow. In a way, this takes the heat off you because your job is simply to enforce the rules established by the administration. You will be required to give a student warnings and perhaps contact the parent(s) or guardian(s), or document an attempt to do so, before a referral can be made to remove a student who is difficult in the classroom.

Usually, all disciplinary actions call for a written report. Make sure you keep the needed forms within arm's reach. Once there is some altercation, you will want to maintain fluid motion rather than be seen fumbling around. Remember again: This is a drama that is unfolding that is usually far more interesting than what you have planned for class that day. Keep in mind who is watching. Don't show disgust, frustration, anger, or other negative emotions on your face. Don't let students know that you've been rattled. It is just a game, and you are playing your role.

If you must exile a student from your classroom, do so as quickly and smoothly as you can. Do not raise your voice, even if the student screams at you. Remain infuriatingly unruffled, repeating again: "You are out of control. You must leave. Now. We will talk about this at another time." You will probably need to give the student a hall pass.

If the student refuses to comply—a very rare situation—the first step is to call for reinforcement. Meanwhile, direct the rest of the students to engage in some activity so they aren't frozen in the role of an audience watching a drama unfold. Instruct the class to work with partners or in groups, some activity that increases the energy and noise level and helps them to work off the vicarious stress they will have experienced watching one of their classmates appear humiliated.

In any discipline policy, you must enforce rules consistently, fairly, and dispassionately. This is not personal—it's not about you; it's about teaching the offender, and the rest of the class, about maintaining order and appropriate boundaries for the sake of everyone's safety and comfort.

TAKING ACTION

Taking part in a fight earns an automatic referral to the dean or principal's office in most schools. Both or all participants must be sent. Call for security, or send a reliable student to get support, and caution the other students away from the fight for their safety. Get help; do not try to break up a fight yourself: You may get hurt. Many well-intentioned teachers, even those who are quite large and strong, have ended up quite bruised, physically and emotionally, when they have tried to break up fights on their own. In some cases, the student(s) might even turn on you.

The unruly student—the one whose parents you've talked to three times, the one you've warned three times in class, the one who steps over the line with her distractions— will have to be exiled to the dean's or principal's office if you are to continue instruction successfully. Take time to write the referral carefully. Many people will see your description of the situation. Use legible handwriting with attention to grammar and spelling. A copy of the form will become part of the student's discipline folder.

You will have a couple of choices to make in how to handle the situation. You can call the student to your desk, or you can walk over to him or her. Be prepared for the student to act out in some way. She may read the referral out loud. She may protest unfair treatment. She may promise to be good and stop talking. Hold your ground. It will be over in a minute. The student will leave, the noise will subside, and you will be able to resume the activities you planned for the period.

If you are suspicious about whether the student will show up at the office, send an escort along. If the student refuses to go, call for help. Schools have students log in their arrival times to keep track of them. Follow up at the end of the day to see that the student did sign the log and what consequences were implemented by the dean or principal. This will also allow you to check to see if other teachers have been having trouble with the same student. If that is the case, you may wish to consult with colleagues to coordinate some future action to prevent other problems.

After the altercation itself, you may wish to discuss the matter with the class, if that is appropriate and there is some lesson to be learned. You do not owe the students an explanation, but sometimes it is helpful for morale to talk about conflict, resolution, and feelings. They have been witness to a "power play." Younger students may need help interpreting the situation, analyzing options, and understanding authority. They may benefit from a brief respite themselves before they are able to turn their attention to their work.

In unusual situations in which you feel emotionally overwhelmed or injured, ask for relief. An administrator, a teacher with a free period, or an aide from another room can come in for a few minutes to give you a break, time to collect your thoughts and feelings and figure out how to approach the students.

PROCESSING THE EXPERIENCE

Conflicts can be viewed as an opportunity for growth. They teach you about your own limits. They underscore issues of power and control. They bring to your attention unresolved issues that you may need to examine more closely. They regulate distance in relationships when one or more parties may feel threatened by intimacy. The important thing is to reflect on what happened during the altercation, what the conflict or disagreement or acting out was really about. Consider the following possibilities:

- The student was after attention and was willing to win it at any cost.
- A power struggle ensued because each of you was determined to win control.
- The student felt disrespected and felt the need to assert him- or herself.
- The student was acting inappropriately, asking for some intervention.
- The student was manipulative, controlling, and game playing, enjoying the challenge of getting underneath your skin.

- Things escalated out of control because the student was asking for direction, structure, or limits that you weren't able or willing to provide.
- The problem behavior was triggered by your asking the student to do something that he or she was unable to do.
- One of your buttons got pushed, and you overreacted.
- The student displaced anger toward you that was really directed elsewhere (a parent or other authority figure).
- You misinterpreted the situation, and the person you disciplined wasn't the primary culprit.

These are just a few of the possibilities. Usually, the situation is so complex that a number of factors are operating, some that involve the student, some that involve others in the class or in the student's life, and some that involve you and your own personal issues related to power and control. Most often, there is some interactive effect operating, and each of the participants in the struggle had some role in its genesis and maintenance.

For you to learn from the experience, you must reflect on what happened, what you did that may have exacerbated the problem, what you could have done differently, and what parts had nothing to do with you whatsoever. This is a very difficult task to undertake alone. It is far better to consult with a colleague to help you unravel the predicament.

A good place to begin in your learning process is to check with the dean or assistant principal who handled the matter. See if there is any background information related to the student's behavior that is relevant to the episode in the classroom. Find out how the situation was resolved in the office. Most important, arrange some time in which you can meet with the student or parents (or both) to debrief the episode and smooth things over for the future. You do not want to be stuck with an enemy in your class who is committed to revenge and payback for some perceived injustice.

Unfortunately, with some kids, there is little you can do to put things behind you. He or she enjoys the power that comes from remaining obstinate and disruptive, from challenging authority figures; the acting out becomes intrinsically rewarding for the student no matter what you do. With some cases, you will just have to accept the limits of what is within your control. It does take two committed parties to heal a rift. Whatever happens, you must let go of things and move on. Almost every week, if not every day, there will be some similar episode. You must develop your own ways to handle and process these struggles, to not take them personally; they simply come with the job. No sense in complaining about them too much (as some teachers do); that doesn't change things either and will only make you bitter. Accept the reality that in almost any class you teach, there will be a few individuals who are singularly unpleasant—no different than anywhere else in the world where there are always a few people who seem to thrive on making others' lives as difficult as they can.

WHEN THE STUDENT RETURNS

Whether a private conference with the offending student has taken place or not, there will be a critical time when he or she returns to your class. This could occur the next day, in a few days, or even the following semester.

You will want to avoid future repetitions of the same problem. At the same time, you want to reconnect with the student in such a way that you both can forgive, forget, and move forward. It is truly amazing, sometimes, how your best relationships with kids will evolve from these conflicts.

I (Jeffrey) worked with one student who was my worst nightmare. He had a smart mouth. He was always questioning things, and he couldn't seem to sit still for long, always in motion. Truth be told, he was a lot like me.

Initially, I tried to bring him under control, but to no avail. I tried everything I could think of to stop him from being disruptive in class. Nothing worked. I consulted with many colleagues to get advice, but perhaps this young man had his own confidants as well: Every time I came in with some new discipline strategy, he would change his own approach. He always seemed to be a step ahead of me.

We butted heads throughout the year. I spent an embarrassing amount of time thinking about him, feeling inept and incompetent. It felt like he saw through me, that he knew I was a fraud, that I didn't really know what I was doing. Actually, a part of me secretly admired him because he was confident and assertive.

In time, I came to really value this boy's contributions to my class. He remained slippery and unpredictable, at times even incorrigible. I never did develop any consistent discipline plan to bring him under control. But over time, that didn't seem to matter much. We eventually developed a deep respect for one another, to the point where he actually became my favorite student. The turning point for me was confronting my own need to beat him in this battle of wills.

When the student does return to your class after being sent to the office or suspended, try to make sure the reentry is as comfortable as possible. Let the student know if the seating in the classroom has been changed. Inform the student about what topic is being covered. Be attentive without being solicitous. Try to structure things in such a way that you can avoid future confrontations.

RESPECT

I (Cary) think teachers should find a balance in the ways they discipline. The best way to keep students from acting out is to make them respect you by setting specific expectations. If I respect my teacher a lot, then I'm not going to create many problems.

One teacher was just too nice. She made threats, but she never carried them out. She didn't do what she said she would. Over and over, students would do crazy things and she was powerless to stop anyone. Everyone took her as a joke. Nobody really learned much in that class. We liked the teacher, but we didn't respect her.

Respect is a two-way street. The teacher must also take into consideration the feelings and needs of the students in the room. Teenagers react well to reasonable explanations. The language you use to speak to the students, as well as your tone of voice, send potent messages to the class. An initial discussion of class rules and the school discipline policy, combined with conscientious planning and thorough preparation on your part, will limit the opportunities difficult students will have to test you.

13

Getting Involved in Activities

O n one hand, you will have plenty to do just staying on top of your assigned classes. The last thing you need as a brand-new teacher is added responsibilities and commitments at school. On the other hand, some of the most enjoyable and satisfying interactions you will ever have with students will take place not in the traditional classroom but in extracurricular activities related to school clubs and sports, competitions, and career and social organizations.

Although it would be far better for you to get involved slowly in various school activities (especially if you are going through an induction program), possibly even waiting until your second or third year on the job, an opportunity may arise that is too enticing to pass up: A coach or club adviser unexpectedly quits, and you are invited to take over the group. The principal approaches you with an invitation to begin or continue a particular school organization, and it wouldn't look good for you to turn it down. Or perhaps you just have this burning desire to make a difference in kids' lives in a setting that isn't as restrictive as the traditional classroom.

Activity Adviser

The things teachers most dislike about their classroom jobs are that they are constantly called on to keep students on track, to evaluate their performances, and to keep order and discipline. Furthermore, the participants in a classroom are not often volunteers; they have not really chosen to be in your classes. In the case of extracurricular activities, students *choose* to devote their own time to participate in the enterprise. Although some students have hidden or disguised agendas not related to true devotion to the activity, they still have a degree of motivation that prevents most discipline problems. For instance, even those students who are participating in debate or a community service organization for less than altruistic reasons—because they want to beef up their resumes, please their parents, or hang out with friends—are still there voluntarily.

School clubs provide a range of enrichment activities that allow students to pursue personal interests, such as dance clubs, drama clubs, science clubs, or future teachers clubs. Often, they take field trips. Frequently, they invite speakers to their meetings. Most schools have a wide variety of service clubs, some of them related to those in the community at large. For example, the Kiwanis organization supports Key Clubs in many areas of the country. Not only do students participate in many hours of community service work but they also have an opportunity to gain valuable leadership experience.

Your role as the adviser to a club is to keep the students on task, provide some organizational skills and references, and help students with their planning. Meanwhile, you have the chance to get to know students in a more informal way. As a result of your efforts, you not only will get to see the difference you are making in the lives of the students for whom you serve as a resource, but you will also be contributing to and witnessing the maturation process of the students you are mentoring.

School clubs also provide a number of social opportunities for students. For those who are not involved in organized sports or who don't have jobs after school, many teenagers end up having too much unstructured time. Kids sit anesthetized in front of the television, or play video games, or sleep all afternoon. Even worse, drugs and alcohol are used as means to deal with boredom and stress.

For me (Cary), everything I remember most fondly about high school took place outside of class. I hate to be the one to tell teachers this because they think what they do is so important. But the most fun I had, and probably the most stuff I learned, occurred when I was involved in all the extracurricular activities. I played on the baseball team for four years and learned everything I know about teamwork and self-discipline and commitment and dealing with pressure situations.

I remember once seeing one of my teachers at a game, watching me pitch. It was a teacher I hadn't really respected much or paid much attention to before, but just seeing him at the game made a big difference to me. After that I started to listen to him more and actually learned some things from him that I would not have otherwise.

I was also on the Student Council and that taught me a lot of things, too, none of which was expected. I thought I'd learn about leadership and social activism, but what I learned about was how to deal with authorities. Still, it was a far more powerful lesson than anything I could have ever learned in class.

The reality of contemporary life is that there just aren't many places that teenagers can go after school. They may hang out at malls or convenience stores. They roam around the streets looking for something to do. Boredom, or just plain lack of stimulation and structure, is a very real problem in most kids' lives. That is where school activities can serve a really useful purpose—providing structure, useful things for kids to do, chances to interact with others around a common purpose, and the opportunity to make new friends.

As an adviser to school clubs and organizations, you get to do things *with* students rather than plan for them. You are not so much an authority figure as you are a wise, older adviser who helps them solve their own problems.

The activities of clubs are shared learning experiences based on common interests. Often, the teacher and students do things together for the first time—going on a field trip, for example. Common bonds are built, where you will later hear, "Remember when we . . ." Students have the opportunity to observe you in a new way and see your reactions to novel situations.

Another advantage of sponsoring a club is that you get to meet students who are not in your classes. Getting to know more people will help you feel more comfortable in the school. You will become aware of the school's social patterns and see who is friends with whom. You will watch as attachments form among the boys and girls, and you will see how new students are drawn into various groups.

CLASS SPONSOR

Being a class sponsor is another way to get involved with students. This is certainly a big responsibility at the beginning of the school year. Most schools have homecoming traditions to maintain, including making floats for the homecoming parade. Classes participate in assemblies and pep rallies, hold events for the school, and often engage in fund-raising projects. Sponsoring a class is another chance to get to know the students and work with them outside the classroom.

Regardless of what activity you choose to help with, you will have opportunities to develop relationships outside that of the traditional "teacher-student," and you will increase the rapport you have with your students.

COACHING ATHLETICS

Although coaching a sport leads to evaluations of performance, like the classroom, it also provides another venue for teacher-student interaction. Students are intensely motivated to participate in and/or be selected for school sports teams. They know their abilities will be assessed and are willing to be scrutinized.

Intense relationships develop because of the time, energy, and concentration involved. As a coach, your words may be revered. Students rely on your guidance, your decisions. They know coaches look out for their welfare—making sure they maintain good grades and develop good fitness habits. You share your expertise. Students see you in a different light as you make on-the-spot decisions. In this environment, students are often willing to hear criticism if it will lead to improvement.

Coaches may work with the same students over several years. They have the opportunity to see the players grow and develop as they mature into young men and women. In the role of coach, you foster camaraderie, a strong work ethic, and team spirit. You teach physical and social skills, build self-esteem and confidence, and create an esprit de corps in which cooperation is valued over individual accomplishment. You teach the value of practice and self-discipline and help students overcome injury, errors, and defeat. You help kids develop poise and dignity, whether they win or lose, and you see bonds develop that will last the rest of their lives.

When I (Cary) was playing baseball, my coach ran my life. I was with him more than I was with my own father. I ran hard every day at practice. I lifted weights until I could no longer feel my arms. I never worked so hard at anything in my life, and I can't imagine there will ever be a time that I will work harder. Even if I wanted to get into trouble, there wasn't any time to do so. I used to leave for school at 6:30 in

*the morning, and I didn't get home until 6:00. Even my
weekends were filled with practices. And we're talking
11 months per year.*

*The lessons my coach taught us weren't just about base-
ball but about life. It's about working together toward
achieving one goal. Every day, 3 or 4 hours of practice.
Sometimes, even 5 or 6 hours, in the intense heat or the
bitter cold.*

*My coach scared the crap out of me sometimes, but I
respected him as much as I've respected any man. He has
played a large part in making me who I am. All of my time
that he took up every day was his time, too. He has devoted
his whole life to helping kids like me. He receives very little
extra pay and not nearly enough recognition.*

HONORING SCHOOL TRADITIONS

Even if you don't have the time and inclination to actually
sponsor a club or coach an athletic team, you can still become
involved in after-school activities by attending and promoting
important events, such as school dances, games, and school
performances.

Every school has its own customs, and some of the more
typical traditions follow. Many schools have spirit day every
Friday. The first round of school spirit activities usually
comes during the homecoming season, with a "spirit week"
organized around a theme. Each class and many clubs build
floats for the homecoming parade before the game. Each day
of the week may have a special designation for dress. Samples
might include College Day—wear your favorite college
T-shirt or sweatshirt; Hat Day—wear the cap or hat of your
favorite sports team; Stripe Day; Plaid Day; '60s Day; Disney
Character Clothing Day; and so forth. Although they won't
often admit it, students do appreciate it when teachers get into
the spirit of things.

School dances at both the middle or junior high school and high school level attract a lot of student attention. As invitations go out, some hearts will rise, others will fall. Sometimes, the invitations will be quite creative—a balloon with a message inside; a box with Hershey's kisses, only one of which has a message; a poster that you will be asked to deliver to a student in a class. The answers will be just as clever—a bottle of jelly beans with a note that says "Odd means yes. Even means no."

Each dance may have its own customs as well. In one district, at GR (Girls' Reverse, where the girls invite the boys), the couple wears matching shirts for the evening. Often, there will be a photographer to take pictures of couples and groups of friends. Then, about two weeks later, the pictures will arrive at school, and much student attention will be given to the pictures—how they came out and who gets copies.

October's event commanding attention is Halloween. Will you be in costume? Schools have different policies on dress for teachers and students; some allow modest outfits if they are not considered distracting.

November is marked by food drives around Thanksgiving. Blankets and other needed items may also be collected. Some schools collect toiletries to distribute to the homeless. High school football play-offs take place during this month—rivalries may be bitter. Also, National Education Week is celebrated the third week in November with recognition for teachers that may range from banners in the school or special messages placed in teachers' mailboxes to ice cream parties after school and small gifts of appreciation from students, the school, the district and/or parent organizations.

December may feature a toy drive for underprivileged students. There will likely be orchestra and band concerts. There will also be school assemblies to celebrate the holidays and to acknowledge awards for student achievements.

January is the end of the semester. Most schools do not hold any activities during finals week. Many schools have a Martin Luther King Jr. Day recognition of some kind, and schools are closed to observe the day itself.

February is the time for boys' and girls' high school basketball play-offs. You'll want to also note the extracurricular schedule for sports, performance, and academic competitions. Another high school assembly may be held to honor winter sports.

March is the beginning of spring sports.

April or May is often the time for another spirit week. Sometimes, those who will graduate at the end of the year are honored during this month. More dress-up days may be planned, along with an assembly and after-school activities such as a movie night or barbecue. Participants in spring sports may be acknowledged.

At the high school level, school rings continue to be popular. Students buy them as early as their sophomore year. Many schools have special ring-day celebrations when they are delivered.

The arrival of yearbooks continues to be an exciting day at any level. Many schools have a signing party—which is just like it sounds. The students receive their books and then take turns autographing them after school. This is a fun event to watch and participate in.

The senior year is marked by many rituals—the final homecoming, ordering graduation announcements, being measured for caps and gowns, the last game or meet for the senior athletes, senior pictures, awards night, and of course, the senior prom. Students identify themselves by the year they graduate from high school—tassels with their graduation year are displayed on the rearview mirrors of their cars or trucks, or the year may be painted on the windows.

OTHER TRADITIONS

There can be some negative traditions as well. Incoming freshmen can be the target of jokes and hazing. They are told to use an elevator to get to the second story of a building when there is no elevator, or older students give them incorrect directions. Do be on the lookout for lost freshmen.

There are many alumni traditions as well. Alumni return on career day to share information about their professions with the students. The high school graduates return for the homecoming game, at which alumni band members may play a number and alumni cheerleaders may join in the acrobatics for the playing of the school fight song. At one school, the former graduates spend the day attending an assembly in the morning, then an alumni luncheon, and finally, the game in the evening. Alumni reunions are held every 10 years, if not every 5. When the school vies for a state athletic championship, the alumni will turn out in droves, in their letter sweaters or jackets.

All of these events and traditions may sound a bit confusing, if not overwhelming. Over time, you will decide on what activities you wish to become involved with—as a sponsor, an adviser, a participant, or a spectator. The point is that you fully join the school culture, becoming part of the family, once you devote yourself to some extracurricular activities. Be prepared to spend a little extra money to support the various student activities. I (Ellen) have bought T-shirts, pens, candy, gift wrap, greeting cards, locker mirrors, and key chains to contribute to clubs and athletic programs. Students and administration will appreciate your visible support. And you will find that spending time with students away from your classroom is a wonderful break from the usual routines.

14

Networking With Professionals

Staying connected with students is certainly related to success in your job. However, it is just as important to network with others in your school and the community. You are actually part of a team that delivers coordinated services to students. Because you can't be expected to know and do it all, you can rely on other professionals for support, for students' welfare as well as academic achievement. For this reason, it is important to know what resources are available and how to access them.

SUPPORT SYSTEM

Teachers are members of a helping profession, along with others who are part of the school team: counselors, psychologists, special-education experts, nurses, librarians, media consultants, and a host of others who keep the school running. Your fellow teachers and staff will guide you through forms that have to be completed, field trip permission procedures, fire drills, and acquiring classroom supplies. They will also help you get to know the resources in the community, which is especially important if you have just relocated. They will become a support system for you.

There was an older girl in my (Ellen's) high school, mixed-age Spanish I class who grimly made her way to her seat each day. She knew a few words in the language but was not progressing well. She looked disheveled and tired, with gray splotches under her eyes. She seemed to try and concentrate but never participated in discussions.

After several brief conversations with her, I learned that she worked a steady job in a local restaurant. Not too long ago, this student had been burned while taking pizzas out of the oven. In addition, she had just found out she was pregnant. Furthermore, she had no health insurance and no support from her family. No wonder she had little motivation to learn Spanish!

I realized there was only so much I could do for this young woman. We talked about her situation, and I told her about the community health department resource that I thought might be helpful—to look at her wounds, and explain the implications of her pregnancy and her need for medical care. I also referred her to the school nurse.

In addition, I contacted her school counselor and involved the school social worker, because this student had quite a number of problems related to her family, her boyfriend, and important decisions related to her pregnancy and future plans. As much as the girl seemed to trust me, I knew that I didn't have the time or the proper training to handle this all on my own. I needed help, and I was glad that it was available to relieve my burden—not just the workload, but the emotional stress of caring so much about kids like this girl and feeling like there is so little that I can do on my own.

CONSULTATIONS

There are a number of situations that may present themselves for which you will want to enlist the help of others. If you suspect that one of your students is being physically or sexually abused, or neglected, for example, you must report such observations right away. If you believe a student is in danger of hurting himself or herself, or someone else, you must take immediate action as well. For instances such as these and other presenting issues, you will want to consult with other professionals associated with the school and district.

For various behavior problems you're unable to deal with on your own, there are a number of people you can consult—first of all, the parents of the offending child. Use them as consultants just as you would any other professional available. Talk to your department chair or a more experienced teacher who is willing to mentor you. They may be able to provide some insight if they have had the student in the past or someone with similar behavior. In addition, make use of the following resources as needed:

School Counselor. A great source of help is the guidance counselor. The counselor can call in a student to talk about behavior without any negative repercussions (i.e., the student isn't "in trouble"). A counselor can talk to students in private. Also, you can ask the counselor to come to the classroom and do a general program, for everyone, on communication skills, self-esteem, cooperation, or decision-making skills. If a student comes to you to talk about a problem that makes you uncomfortable—drugs, birth control, pregnancy—or you sense a problem situation, such as abuse or neglect, then conferring with the counselor will help you determine whether to make a referral for the student to see the counselor directly. As a transition to having the student meet one-on-one with the counselor, the three of you might talk together first.

One other function counselors serve is as consultants for teachers. Feel free to talk to a counselor you trust about some of your own doubts and concerns or as a way to deal with your own stress. As an ex-counselor and current counselor educator, let me (Jeffrey) reassure you that one of the best parts of our job is working with teachers directly. I really appreciated it when teachers came to me for advice or support. Motivated teachers are a pleasure to work with.

Administration. Likewise, you can ask a dean or an assistant principal to intervene on your behalf and talk to a student, without initiating a formal disciplinary procedure. In addition to the advantage of an outside party acting as a mediator in a conflict, such a person offers the benefit of a private office where he or she and the student can talk without fear of interruption or a class change.

Other Teachers. Talk to other teachers as much as you can. Find out how the problem child behaves in other classes. If you work as part of a team, perhaps someone else can speak to the child on your behalf. This will send a message to the student that everyone is aware of his or her behavior, that everyone is paying attention to him or her, and they expect improvement.

School Psychologist. If there are truly serious problems with behavior, then a referral will likely need to be made to the school psychologist or someone in the community—a physician for medication review, a psychologist for regular therapy, or some other specialist who can deliver the kind of intensive, individualized service that may be required. It isn't your job to make these direct referrals on your own, but it is a good idea to know what options and services are available, should the need arise.

Special Education Facilitator. If you feel a student has serious academic or emotional problems, there will be a referral procedure for you to follow, beginning with forms to fill out that require observation and descriptions and/or examples of the student's behavior and work. The next step may be referral to a screening committee made up of school personnel. There will be an informational meeting with the student's parent(s) or guardian(s). Permission for testing will be required. It may take some time before the testing can be scheduled, and then the results will have to be evaluated. Additional meetings will be held with the parent(s) or guardian(s). If at this point it is discovered that the student does have a special need, then an individual education plan (IEP) will be written by a team with a lead special-education teacher.

The IEP will take into account the abilities of the student. Specific objectives will be identified with accommodations and modifications noted. The special-education teacher will be able to suggest strategies for you to use to accomplish the objectives for which you would be responsible. You will need to make adjustments in the learning expectations and assessments, and extra help may be made available to the student. If support is warranted, the student may have the opportunity to go to a resource room during your class period, or the resource teacher will be able to come to your room to help. Both instances require good communication between the classroom teacher and the resource teacher.

Nurse. It's surprising how often you may come into contact with the school nurse and health aide(s). For various health emergencies—a student fainting or having a seizure, for example—you will need to immediately contact the health office and/or the principal. If the situation is one of great risk, other emergency medical service people will be called. Injuries that occur in physical education, such as a twisted ankle that later swells up, might not show up until your class. Medical emergencies, such as asthma or serious allergy attacks, may take place in your room. In each of these cases, you must take appropriate steps to make sure the student receives proper medical care. Most schools provide teachers with a list of students who have reported medical problems, from epilepsy to bee sting allergies, so they can be monitored. The information will also tell what to do and whom to contact if these situations arise.

Librarian. The school librarian will be a great resource for you as well for academic concerns. Not only does he or she know the interests and ability levels of the students, but will also be able to match materials to their needs and interests. In addition, the librarian's relationships with students will be very different from yours, as he or she maintains contact with the students over 3 or 4 years and can get to know them very well. Frequently, the librarian is also responsible for the audiovisual materials, including videotapes and laser discs, as well as CDs and DVDs. He or she will be able to make recommendations for electronic and print references for you and your students, depending on what you are looking for.

Curriculum Specialists. Many districts have curriculum specialists in the central office. Their responsibilities typically include curriculum development, textbook adoption, and professional development in the content area. They are often available to meet individually with new teachers to provide curriculum support—teaching strategies—and acquaint you with resources. They will help you develop lessons that are interesting and relevant for students, captivating and keeping their attention, reducing or eliminating the need for further discipline problems.

Other Specialists. Consultants are also available to you in the area of technology. A computer specialist or information technology (IT) resource person, for example, will most likely be able to help you with software programs and/or hardware problems that arise. Such a person may even provide you with periodic targeted training.

Another valuable person is the learning strategist, if your district has one. The function of this person is to provide support and help teachers develop the resources needed to teach a particular concept. They may demonstrate a lesson or present methods and materials to the classroom teacher. In addition, they may help the teacher evaluate learning styles. The strategist may come from one of many backgrounds, such as literacy or technology.

TEAM TEACHING

If you are not already assigned to a team, consider organizing one yourself. There are many wonderful interdisciplinary projects that can challenge your students if you coordinate your lessons with people in other fields. From studying earthquakes to the Middle Ages, teachers can work together to coordinate their efforts. Set times for planning together. Consult about your time schedules for student tests and projects. Divide the evaluation chores evenly so no one feels overburdened. Keep the communication lines open. Even if you just work with another teacher in your field, you can combine your efforts and learn from one another, and the students will only benefit.

PARAPROFESSIONALS

With the mainstreaming of special-needs students in the classroom, more schools have paraprofessional educators available to help classroom teachers. As a result, you may have an adult in your classroom, under your supervision, who will be able to work directly with students. While this may seem like an overwhelming responsibility in the beginning, as time goes on, you will see great benefits.

As in any collaborative relationship, you will need to spend some time when you first meet this person to get to know his or her strengths and resources, as well as limitations. Find out what types of experience he or she brings to the classroom. If the aide has a history in the school and the community, this paraprofessional can also serve as a resource to explain school traditions and procedures, as well as identify resource people for you. They may have seen effective teaching in the past and will be able to make constructive suggestions, if you are open to them. Be sure to arrange a set meeting time each week to go over your lesson plans and discuss how and when the paraprofessional will interact with the students. Open communication will help assure a healthy working relationship.

In your initial discussion, explain your philosophy of education, your discipline policy, and what routines you will establish. Clarify with the paraprofessional exactly what his or her duties will be and what authority he or she has. You may need to provide some instruction as to how to best interact with the students and how to implement your discipline policy. You may need to review IEPs together. The paraeducator will be able to spend time during class reviewing and reinforcing vocabulary, concepts, and skills you present, as well as help with individual assignments. Help the person feel welcome in your room by providing work space—a desk or table—in your room, and giving him or her a copy of your text and instructional materials.

Districts vary as to the type of responsibilities given to paraeducators and the role they play as part of an educational team, so you will need to follow the guidelines in your school. While you may be tempted to have the paraprofessional take care of clerical and copying tasks, that would not be appropriate. Increased professional development opportunities are becoming available for paraprofessionals as well, so be sure to pass on such information and encourage participation. Also, you will want to find out what the current union policies are, especially with respect to hours of work, break times, and job responsibilities.

WORKING WITH PEOPLE IN THE COMMUNITY

To add academic richness and diversity to your class, recruit people from the community to visit your students. Retired persons, for example, are often hungry for opportunities to share their lifelong expertise. Bring in guest speakers, arrange for demonstrations, and put on performances. Professional organizations and businesses usually have lists of speakers and presentations available for school children. Check to see if your school already has established partnerships in the community. Media people may be willing to visit your classroom to talk about relevant issues. Draw on experts and resources from the local universities. Most important, make a point of involving parents as contributors.

YOU ARE NOT ALONE

The important thing to remember, as a beginning teacher, is that you are not alone. There are a number of formal channels in place that can provide you with support and networking to do your job and deal with any challenges that arise. Informal networking is also invaluable, not only to help you deal with immediate problems but also to continue your own growth and education as a professional.

15

Using a Substitute

"Are you a sub?"
"What are we going to do today?"
"Do we have to sit in our seats?"
"Are we going to have the test tomorrow?"
"Where is our teacher?"
"When is our teacher going to be back?"

Just so you know, any time I (Cary) walk into class and see a substitute sitting by your desk, I rub my hands together and think to myself, "It's time to play." Having a sub means we're probably not going to be doing any work. Unless you include picture identification cards, students are going to trade names and seats. They will try to bend any rule they can. It's open season.

Try to avoid having the sub teach anything because they usually have no idea what they are talking about. Just give an assignment for the kids to work on and turn in at the end of the period. Other than that, just hope that things don't get too far out of control.

OF NECESSITY

There will come a time when you will need to be absent from school. You may be sick, have a doctor's appointment, attend a professional development program or an IEP conference, or take a personal day for one reason or another. In any event, when you are not going to be in class, arrangements will have to be made for a substitute. The secret is to be prepared.

The procedures for arranging a substitute vary from one district to another. In one place, you may contact the substitute yourself; in another, you will contact a secretary who makes the call; in yet a third, you may telephone information to a Touch-Tone system. Usually, you will have the opportunity to state a preference for a particular person to be your sub.

MEETING SUBSTITUTES

In most districts, there will be substitutes who are well acquainted with the staff, policies, and students of the school. They will be known by the students. As a new teacher, it would be beneficial to make a point to meet these people. One opportunity to do this is in the morning, in the secretary or office manager's office, when substitutes check in. You can find out a little about their backgrounds and their experience. Another chance to talk to substitutes will be when you see them in your hallway or in the classroom next door. You may also come into contact with them at breaks or lunchtimes. Make it a point to welcome them; you know what it feels like to be a newcomer.

Other teachers may make recommendations for you. There may be times when you have to call on someone you don't know. Whether or not you have met the substitute ahead of time, there are several things you can do to facilitate a smooth transition.

Providing Information

In preparation for an absence, whether it is anticipated or not, it is helpful to gather information together for the substitute. A suggested format can be found at the end of this chapter. In one school district in South Carolina, the high school required that information for substitutes be kept in a folder in the teacher's mailbox at all times. Whether you are provided with a folder or make up your own, the following points will be beneficial for anyone who takes over your classroom.

First, the substitute will need to know the correct spelling of your name, your room number(s), and the bell schedule. If your school has standard assembly or short-day schedules, a copy of these should be included, too. Although the substitute may receive a copy of the school map on arrival, it would be nice to include a map of the school with your room(s) clearly indicated, along with the nearest fire alarm, exit, bathroom, principal's or dean's office, and teachers' lounge.

For each period, provide general information about your classes: course title, course description, textbook(s). The substitute will need rosters of your students. You will need to update this list periodically to include additions and deletions. Likewise, try to maintain up-to-date seating charts in this file. If you have access to a digital camera, you can print out pictures of your students to help the substitute learn their names.

Many teachers will leave a list of names of students who can advise a substitute on class procedures. It is a good idea to leave several names for each period in case the first student on the list is also absent that day. Specific information on the lesson plan can follow. If you know in advance that you will be absent, you can also include a list of students who are scheduled to be absent that day due to field trips or participation in other school activities.

You may decide to prepare an all-purpose lesson that can be used at any time during the year. This will relieve any anxiety that you may feel when it becomes apparent that you will not be able to attend school as planned. Place the substitute's lesson plan in an obvious place, such as on your desk, in the top drawer of your desk, or on the file cabinet or book shelf close to your desk. Write a reference to the plan's location in your substitute folder as well. It would be a good idea to let your neighbor teachers and your department chair know where the substitute's lesson plan will be, as well, because these are the people the substitute will turn to for help if he or she cannot find it. Once this plan is used, you will need to create another one.

Class procedures should be carefully described. You may have special activities that are performed each day, such as a current events discussion, a geography question, a thought for the day, or the writing of a journal entry. Perhaps you follow a special dismissal policy. Anything you would like to see continued in your absence will have to be specified for the substitute.

Substitutes will also need information related to specific students. In this category, you will need to list students with special medical problems and the courses of action to follow. Disabilities would be noted. You would acknowledge students who need to leave early or are permitted to arrive late. Any student who is an aide would also be listed.

Special duties you have will need to be highlighted. For example, if you are responsible for hall duty at a particular place and time, this would be indicated. Let the substitute know if you have a university practicum teacher or a student teacher. The substitute will be the responsible teacher in these situations, not the practicum or student teacher (his or her responsibilities are usually limited to the times when the classroom teacher of record is present). Their roles need to be clarified for all parties involved.

Leave any necessary supplies in a conspicuous place or note where they can be found. If audiovisual equipment is needed, reference this as well as where and how to obtain the equipment. Because students will use as an excuse the fact that they don't have pencil or paper to do an assignment, it will make the substitute's life easier if you leave a small reserve supply. Also, to make sure the students use the class time as intended, develop an assignment that is due at the end of the period. This does not have to be a formal project or writing assignment; it can be a brainstorming of ideas, a three-sentence summary, a picture—whatever you decide. If possible, develop something that is reasonably fun so that students will not create unnecessary discipline problems.

The substitute will need access to your school forms: The attendance will have to be reported. He or she may need to write a pass for a student. On occasion, he or she will have to write a discipline referral. Also, it is a good idea to leave paper on which the substitute can report on the students' behavior, as well as how and to what extent your plan was followed. In some schools, the substitute will need to submit this information to the office on a specific form.

Students will want to know why you are absent and how long you will be away. If you are comfortable providing this information to the substitute and letting him or her disclose it, you will prevent a barrage of questions and help reduce the anxiety level of the classroom while you are away. Furthermore, if your absence will constitute a change in their schedule, such as a new test date, presentation schedule, or project deadline, an announcement by the substitute would be beneficial and timely as well, so be sure to ask the substitute to convey this to the class. The more the students' welfare is considered, the smoother the transitions of your absence and your return will be.

SUBSTITUTE LESSON PLANS

With respect to writing a lesson plan, keep the educational flow going as much as possible while creating a meaningful experience for the students. Structure activities that are consistent with the unit of study. Write objectives that the substitute can communicate to the students so that they will know what the expectations are for the period. The students should be informed as to what will be required of them and what they need to do to stay on task. This communication will provide for the best use of time for students as well as the substitute. Consider creating a plan that will involve the substitute as a resource person for the students. If you know the substitute has an area of expertise or an interesting life story that relates to your content area, you might request that he or she share this with the class. For example, a retired policeman might have a wealth of knowledge on laws and examples of how they are applied that would be applicable to a civics class. Discuss the topic and story ahead of time with the substitute to ensure the content is appropriate for the age level of your students and relates to your lesson.

Encourage the substitute to introduce himself or herself to the class. It is important that the students get to know the alternate who is responsible for them for the day. In some ways, having a guest teacher can energize the classroom in ways that wouldn't otherwise be possible. Much depends on the quality of the professional you select for the temporary assignment and how well you have prepared that person to do the job. The following are sample forms for providing information to the substitute (Form 15.1) and for a substitute's report back to you (Form 15.2).

Form 15.1   Information for Substitute Teacher

Teacher's Name _____   Room(s) _____

Schedule:

Period	Class	Textbook	Time	Room
_____	_____	_____	_____	_____
_____	_____	_____	_____	_____
_____	_____	_____	_____	_____
_____	_____	_____	_____	_____
_____	_____	_____	_____	_____
_____	_____	_____	_____	_____
_____	_____	_____	_____	_____
_____	_____	_____	_____	_____

Special duties: _____

Student roster: attached or in folder
Seating chart: attached or in folder

Nearest fire alarm _____
Signal for fire alarm _____
Nearest exit for fire alarm drill _____
Other emergency procedures: _____
_____
_____

Students with special needs:

Name	Period	Need
_____	_____	_____
_____	_____	_____
_____	_____	_____
_____	_____	_____
_____	_____	_____

Student helpers:

Period	Name
_____	_____
_____	_____
_____	_____
_____	_____
_____	_____
_____	_____
_____	_____
_____	_____

Helpful teachers:

Name	Room
_____	_____
_____	_____

Location of lesson plans: _____

Location of supplies: _____

Include: __ Map
            __ Assembly schedule
            __ Excused absence list for field trip or activity
               participation
            __ Hall passes
            __ Discipline referral forms

Form 15.2   Substitute Teacher Report

Class_____

Student Absences _____

_____

Student Tardies _____

_____

_____

Lesson Plan Report _____

_____

_____

_____

_____

_____

Student Behavior _____

_____

_____

_____

_____

_____

Comments and Suggestions _____

_____

_____

_____

_____

_____

16

Taking Care of Yourself to Minimize Stress

One of the most difficult aspects of your first year as a teacher is feeling so vulnerable in your probationary position. It is not unduly paranoid of you to feel like everyone is watching you, critically evaluating your performance. In fact, your students, colleagues, and the administration *are* watching closely to see if you have the right stuff to make it in this profession.

BEING EVALUATED

As a student teacher or beginning teacher, your work in the classroom will be evaluated many, many times. Most districts have a policy in which you are regularly observed during the first year, perhaps three of which observations will be the focus of formal, written assessments of your performance.

Initially, this is an unnerving experience, knowing there is someone in your room who is watching every move you make, forming impressions about your competence and worthiness as a teacher. It seems like the people evaluating you walk in at the beginning or middle of a lesson, stay a few minutes, and then leave. You feel like they don't see the whole picture. Much of this stress can be alleviated if you prepare yourself ahead of time, rehearsing the things you will do and say once you are subjected to scrutiny. Of course, you can't always control what happens in your class on a given day. Administrators realize this, which is why they return so many times to give you the benefit of the doubt, especially on those days when it seems you are not functioning at your full potential.

Some things *are* within your control, regardless of how the students act or how well a particular unit goes. Keep an upbeat attitude. Work from a position of strength. Be prepared. Keep your lesson plans and seating charts up to date. Always have an alternate idea in mind in case your timing is off, a lesson is completed sooner than you anticipated, or students fail to comprehend an important point and are not ready to move on to the next step. Maintain your grade book on a regular basis, averaging grades frequently.

It's perfectly natural to feel nervous when an administrator enters the room. My secret (Ellen's) is to take a deep breath, welcome the person, and help him or her find a place to sit (not always an easy task). Next, I provide the visitor with a copy of the book or resource materials I'm using. Sometimes, I give the observer my copy and I share with a student. This gives me time to gain my composure. Then, I continue with my plan.

Some administrators will visit for an entire class period. Others will check in on your class at the beginning, the middle, and the end—and not necessarily in that order. Don't worry that they have missed your opening activity if they walk in during the middle of a session. They may ask you about it at a later time, or perhaps they are looking at another area of your teaching. Most of them have teaching experience, and if you are performing in a competent manner, they do not necessarily stay very long.

Communicate informally with your administrators, as well, especially your evaluator, about what is going on in your classes. These days, most administrators have hall duty and lunch duty. Find out where their assignments are and visit with them from time to time. Invite them to see your room or to stop by at a particular time when you have something special planned that would be of interest to them.

THINGS TO EXPECT

As in most things in life, you can considerably reduce the stress of being evaluated if you know what to expect. Familiarize yourself with the evaluation forms that are used by your administration. Ask to see samples (with names deleted) of evaluations that are particularly glowing as well as those that are deficient. Before you are subjected to formal evaluation by an administrator, ask an experienced colleague to visit your class and give you preliminary feedback. This can act as a dress rehearsal for the real thing, and you can get used to being observed while you work.

The beginning of the school year is a very busy time for everyone. Most administrators do not observe during the first couple of weeks. They will give you time to get to know your students, institute your policies, and set up your routines. If you are not informed by the teacher's manual or during your orientation when the evaluation deadlines are, you can ask the other teachers or your department chair. Perhaps you will notice when the administrators are walking around the building with their notebooks. You can anticipate a visit soon thereafter.

Some districts inform you ahead of time that you will be formally observed. If you have a test scheduled for that day, let the administrator know. You need to be observed in action, demonstrating your energy, your skill, your content knowledge base, and your rapport with the students. Some presentations are more reflective than others of what you do in a classroom.

Inform your students that administrators may be coming to observe the class so they don't overreact to the visit. Under the best of circumstances, they will cooperate in such a way as to show you at your best. Most secondary students are used to administrators visiting in the classroom.

The review of the observation will generally take place a day or more after the visit. Most supervisors will write a narrative description of the behavior as well as complete a checklist. Districts often include "directions for the future" no matter how good you are, so don't be put off by a list of "charges." It may be a recommendation to continue a particular teaching strategy, monitor student behavior, or get involved in extracurricular activities. As a novice, expect a critical review. Some administrators believe they aren't doing their jobs properly if they can't find fault with some things you do, no matter how small it seems to you. Use the comments constructively.

Most evaluation forms require that you sign them, indicating you have read what is included. You are given an opportunity to respond if you like, but be careful that you aren't perceived as defensive or unwilling to accept feedback. Try to be gracious and grateful for whatever feedback the administrators offered.

OTHER SOURCES OF STRESS

Although being evaluated is one source of stress in your life, it is hardly the only one (see Table 16.1). Teaching is a physically and mentally demanding profession. Every day is different. You are constantly on your feet, under the gun, making quick decisions, responding to one situation after another. Mistakes and misjudgments are inevitable. You will need to be forgiving with yourself and your limitations; after all, you *are* a beginner.

In addition to the self-inflicted stress caused by your own unrealistic expectations and fears of failure, there are also

Table 16.1   Sources of Stress

Student-induced Stress	Work Environment-related Stress
angry outbursts	time pressures
accusations of incompetence	school politics
dysfunctional behavior	unreasonable rules
withdrawal	non-supportive peers
parental meddling	supervisory incompetence
student dropouts	excessive paperwork
poor performance	torn allegiances
Self-induced Stress	*Event-related Stress*
perfectionism	legal actions
ruminating about others	money pressures
need for approval	major life transition (divorce, emotional depletion, relocation, etc.)
self-doubt	change in job responsibilities
physical exhaustion	economic cutbacks
unhealthy life style	physical illness
excessive responsibility for students' welfare	world events (war, famine, terrorism)

those related to the profession itself. You are overworked and underpaid. You have far too many students in your classes and far too much work to complete within the time available. It's difficult to prioritize.

The politics in your school can eat you alive. Common to any human organization, gossip can be treacherous. Backbiting, infighting, and building coalitions in times of conflict are routine. Administrators are often less supportive than most teachers would prefer. They have their own pressures to face, with limited budgets and resources and multiple demands on their time.

Some students will be a source of stress in your life. They will haunt you at night, invade your dreams, as well as preoccupy your waking moments. At times, you will feel helpless and frustrated, wondering why some students treat you so poorly and are so unappreciative of your best efforts to help them. Some parents, as well, will attempt to make your life miserable. They will blame you for their children's problems and hold you responsible for every misfortune in their lives. Sometimes, they will speak to you in ways that are rude, disrespectful, and hostile. All of this can take bites out of your soul.

There is an expression among mental health experts about not allowing others to live in your head "rent free." What this means is that it's hard enough to put up with abusive individuals at school. What you do with those events afterward is completely up to you. If you choose—and it is a choice—to invite difficult students, parents, colleagues, and administrators to invade your private time, then your stress levels will escalate. If, on the other hand, you accept that being around some annoying people comes with the job and you shrug it off as best you can, you are likely to metabolize struggles and conflicts much easier.

Some schools are simply not very healthy environments. With overcrowded buildings, involuntary "clients," unappreciated staff, inadequate resources, and a pressured atmosphere to improve academic achievement, a certain amount of stress is a given. When morale is low, political fighting is high, administrators are not sensitive to teacher issues, and students are unmotivated and underachieving, your stress load will be even higher.

We don't mean to discourage you, merely to be realistic about what you can expect. Being realistic will allow you to metabolize problems more easily when they arise. You don't have to get bent out of shape when you hear colleagues complain a lot. You don't have to become unduly upset when you observe teachers being mean or insensitive to one another. You don't have to be surprised when someone works behind the scenes to sabotage you or an angry parent unloads on you. All of this comes with the territory. It doesn't have to be a big deal unless you make it so.

TAKE CARE OF YOURSELF

There are number of things you can do to help yourself deal with the pressures and stress you will face every day.

Write your story. Keep a journal of your first year as a teacher. Talk to yourself on paper every day or at least several times per week. Write about the frustrations you are feeling and what you intend to do about them. Set goals for yourself. Make priorities about things you intend to change. Analyze your own behavior as well as that of the people around you. Confront your own whining and complaining. Force yourself to think positively about what you are doing. Be forgiving of your lapses and mistakes. Try to find some meaning in the struggles you are going through. Learn from what you are living through so you can make yourself stronger and more resourceful in the future.

Structure your days sensibly. Make an appointment with yourself to take care of paperwork. Note deadlines, and iden-tify what information you need to fill out reports. Do the pre-liminaries first, such as reporting tardies and absences and averaging grades. Also, be sure to build in time every day for rest and relaxation. Exercise faithfully. Eat properly. Make sure you have some fun every day.

Prioritize. Not all requests for information must be completed and submitted immediately. Deadlines will vary. Decide which of the many tasks—reports, lesson planning, grading papers—need to be completed first. You might even create a list of when things are due and note on your calendar when you will do them.

Take breaks. Use the time between classes to relax, to chat with a neighbor teacher, and to greet the incoming students. Let yourself enjoy your lunch period.

Be playful. Beginning teachers can be so grim, so overserious. This is important stuff you are doing, but it isn't rocket science in which a single slip will destroy the universe. Try not to take yourself so seriously. Students, in particular, really appreciate teachers who will sometimes loosen up a bit, play with them, and try to create some fun. When you are enjoying your job, then students are more likely to enjoy their learning.

Set realistic goals for yourself. Keep your ambitions high, but realize it will take time to accomplish your goals. As a new teacher, you will need considerable preparation time. With experience, you will become more proficient at what you do and will be able to use your past experiences as a basis on which to improve in the future, rather than constantly inventing new solutions for how best to teach a lesson.

Diversify your life. Structure your lifestyle in such a way that you take time away from teaching to do other things. Hang around non-teachers. Pursue or create interests in other areas so when one aspect of your life isn't going as well as you like, you have others to help you feel fulfilled.

Nourish yourself with love. Surround yourself with others who love and care for you and whom you can love in return. If you don't currently have a supportive family, a loving partner, or enough stimulating friends around, look hard at yourself and what you can do to fill in these gaps. If needed, get some emotional help for yourself in the form of counseling or support groups.

Get enough sleep. People can occasionally forgo food much easier than they can forgo sleep. After school, go home and take a nap. Reenergize for the evening ahead, so you'll have the energy to socialize, pursue other interests, or do school-related work later on.

Teach your friends and family what it means for you to be a teacher. Educate them about the stresses and strains you face every day. Keep them informed about your struggles. Invite them to become part of your teaching world, or they will be left behind.

Leave your personal problems at home. Focus on your students during the workday. If you allow yourself to become distracted and distressed by other issues in your life, you will not only frustrate yourself because you can't do much about them at school, but you will also shortchange your students. If you have some real problems in your life, get some help.

Seek counseling and continued growth. You don't have to have severe problems or major issues to get some help from a professional. Counseling is highly recommended for beginning teachers because of the pressures you experience and the personal changes you undergo. There will be few times in your life when you encounter so many new things about yourself and the world. A counselor can help you make sense of what you are living through and integrate those insights into your work and life.

DEVELOP A SUPPORT GROUP

If your school or district doesn't schedule time for you to meet with other new teachers, arrange to do so on your own. Getting together with other novices will allow you to share your experiences, exchange suggestions for improved practice, and help you see that you are not alone in your experiences. As mentioned above, emphasize the positive. Stay away from playing "I can top that. Would you believe what happened to me last week?" There will be bad class periods, even some bad days, but there will be good ones, too. Don't let your enthusiasm be crushed. The learning curve is tremendous the first year—Analyze what is working well and how your students are progressing, and make a point of continuing with the strategies that are proving effective. Plan some strictly social activities, too. Plan an early breakfast with the other new teachers. Have a potluck dinner with all of your families.

INTERNET SUPPORT

Many teachers find that electronic bulletin boards and chat rooms provide a convenient means by which to interact with other beginning teachers. If you wake up at 3:00 in the morning alert and ready, you can go online and find other responsive souls. There are always live chat rooms with ongoing conversations and scheduled topics. You can also find archived discussions. Participants post questions and receive answers related to teaching specific content, developing relationships with mentors, responding to administration, ideas for lessons, and so on. They share personal examples, offer support, and give feedback. These are ongoing professional discussions you can benefit from, and all you need is a computer and an Internet connection.

You will find there are predictable phases that new teachers experience along with the daily and weekly ups and downs. In August, there is the excitement of obtaining the new position. By the end of September, teachers begin to feel overwhelmed by all the expectations from students, parents, and administrators, and move into a survival mode. As the year ends, teachers experience frustration at the lack of time needed to accomplish all they had hoped to do. Then, as the two-week, end-of-the-year vacation takes place, there is time for relaxation, time for friends and family, and time for reflection on what has been accomplished. As the second semester continues, feelings continue to change toward the positive as many procedures become routine and teachers can plan for the rest of the school year. The end of the year tends to be a stimulating time as teachers look back over the first year with pride in their achievements and think about changes they would like to make for the next year. And so, once again they feel the excitement and dedication a new year brings.

Finding Balance

A certain amount of stress in your job is not only normal but desirable. In moderate doses, stress is another word for excitement and activation: it means you care deeply about what you are doing. It is also normal to worry a bit about what you are doing, and how you are doing it; remember, you are facing a new set of challenges every day. Your job, however, is to keep the level of stress within manageable limits so it does not significantly deprive you of sleep or reasonable peace of mind. If you find yourself in over your head (as you sometimes will), you must ask for help from those you trust. After all, isn't that what you teach your students?

17

Planning for Your Future

Teaching is an ongoing activity that requires continual professional growth; that is, if you want to avoid becoming like some of the burnouts you see going through the motions in your school, counting the months until retirement. Don't kid yourself—once upon a time, they were just like you: Filled with enthusiasm and excitement. Determined to change the world. Convinced they would be different from the older teachers they made fun of. Look at them now.

What distinguishes those teachers who remain passionately committed to their jobs from those who have all but given up is that the former group has worked hard to keep themselves fresh and vibrant. They love what they do because they teach what they love.

If you hope to have a long, distinguished career as a teacher—not as someone who does a credible job but rather as one who strives for excellence—then the seeds for this passion must be planted now. Much depends on who you choose as your mentors, who you surround yourself with as a support system, and how hard you are willing to work on your growth and development. Just like an athlete who works out every day, practices skills religiously, studies new innovations, and keeps himself or herself in peak physical shape, you, too, must devote yourself to superb conditioning—not only of your body but your mind and your spirit as well.

In this book, we have presented constructive advice, from the perspectives of a teacher, a teacher educator, and a student, on what it takes not only to survive your first year in the profession but also to truly flourish. This may help you get through the first year, but what happens after that?

Ironically, in some ways, your first year is the easiest one in the sense that you have no worries about keeping your excitement and enthusiasm at peak levels. Unfortunately, as some teachers gain experience, they also lose some of the spark they once had, the innocence that led them to believe anything was possible.

Right now, you have something very, very precious: your own strong belief that you will be different. You will be the kind of teacher who keeps the momentum going, who continues to commit yourself to future growth, who is always learning, always reinventing yourself. You will be the kind of teacher whom students revere and admire, not just for what you know but for who you are as a human being. Your love and compassion and empathy are transparent, for anyone to see. The kids know how much you care.

This image of the kind of teacher you wish to be can indeed be your reality. Much depends on how committed you remain to following through with your intentions.

BECOME WHAT YOU WISH FOR YOUR STUDENTS

If you want your students to become fearless, constructive risk takers, show them the way by how you lead your own life. If you want them to venture into the unknown, do so yourself. Share the ideas you read about, the new skills you are learning, the travel that has changed your life. Talk about the issues facing the community, the state, the nation. If you would like them to be the kinds of people who are honest, truth seeking, and sincere, then be that yourself. More than anything you say, kids pay attention to who you are.

TRAVEL

There is only so much that you can learn from school and books and movies. See the world or as much of it as you can. Expose yourself to different cultures. Collect stories of your adventures that make your classes come alive. Integrate the pictures you take and the artifacts you bring home into your lessons.

CONTINUING EDUCATION

Most states require continued education as part of an ongoing licensing process. You must receive a certain number of university credits or professional development education credits to recertify. Some school districts offer their own professional development courses. Through continuing education, you will learn new ideas, develop new skills, broaden your knowledge base, and keep abreast of the latest developments in your field.

PROFESSIONAL ORGANIZATIONS

Join teacher organizations on the local, state, and national levels. Your content area professional organization will provide you with social contacts and educational programs. These organizations sponsor annual conferences with sessions on best practices, innovative strategies, how to teach difficult concepts, and integrating technology. Their publications—newsletters and journals—are a great way to keep current

Table 17.1   Professional Organizations

General Professional Organizations	
American Federation of Teachers	www.aft.org
Association for Supervision and Curriculum Development	www.ascd.org
National Board for Professional Teaching Standards	www.nbpts.org/standards
National Education Association	www.nea.org
Phi Delta Kappa	www.pdkintl.org

Specialized Professional Organizations	
American Council for the Teaching of Foreign Languages	www.actfl.org/index/htm
American Alliance for Health, Physical Education, Recreation and Dance	www.aahperd.org
American Alliance for Theater and Education	www.aate.com
American Association of Teachers of French	aatf.utsa.edu
American Association of Teachers of German	www.aatg.org
American Association of Teachers of Spanish and Portuguese	www.aatsp.org
American Choral Directors Association	www.acda.org
Association for the Advancement of Arts Education	www.aaae.org
Council for Exceptional Children	www.ced.sped.org
International Reading Association	www.reading.org
Music Educators National Conference	www.menc.org
National Art Education Association	www.naea-reston.org
National Business Education Association	www.nbea.org
National Council for the Social Studies	www.ncss.org
National Council of Teachers of English	www.ncte.org
National Council of Teachers of Mathematics	www.nctm.org
National Science Teachers Association	www.nsta.org

on issues in the field. Often there are themed issues. The organizations' Web sites also offer excellent resources and references.

NATIONAL BOARD FOR PROFESSIONAL TEACHING STANDARDS

In 1987, the National Board for Professional Teaching Standards was created to establish standards identifying what teachers should know and be able to do. It provides a voluntary system for certifying teachers who meet rigorous standards. Following demonstration of five core propositions, teachers receive National Board Certification that is valid for 10 years and is renewable in one of 24 certificate fields, based on student developmental level(s) and the subject(s) being taught, with more being developed all the time.

As of this writing, there are 23,937 teachers holding National Board Certification across the 50 states, the District of Columbia, and overseas. During 2002–2003, an additional 15,000 teachers applied for this advanced certification. The application process takes place over the course of one school year. Teachers demonstrate their knowledge and skills through performance-based assessments that include a teaching portfolio, videotapes, student work samples, and analysis of the candidate's teaching and student learning. Timed written exercises call for the demonstration of subject area knowledge and how to teach.

In order to qualify, you must have a B.A., a minimum of three years' teaching experience in either public or private school, and a valid state teaching license for those three years. The fee for National Board Certification is $2300. The National Board Scholarship Program was created to make sure that all teachers who want to become candidates for National Board Certification have that opportunity. The resulting certification complements your professional license. In recognition of this accomplishment, many states are offering bonuses of $5,000 for each year a teacher holds a National Board Certification.

REFLECT ON YOUR FUTURE

Do you see yourself staying in the same position in the same school for most of your career? Are there other positions you have in mind, such as coach, administrator, counselor, or school psychologist? Will you sponsor a new club or coach a different sport? Will you turn to another area of education, curriculum development, or administration? Will you share your expertise with others as presenters at conferences? Will you write articles for a professional journal? Are you interested in research? Will you teach at a local university?

Do you want to teach abroad for a period of time? If so, there are a number of opportunities for exchanges, teaching in American schools abroad, and brief sojourns organized by various organizations.

LOOK FOR CHANGE

Teachers who thrive in the profession are those who keep themselves fresh and energized. They keep abreast of developments in their fields. They are constantly tinkering with their methods. They make changes in the ways they operate. They seek new ways to reach children more effectively.

One way to avoid boredom, burnout, and cynicism is to look for changes you can make in what you teach, how you teach, and where you teach. You can change grade levels or specialties. You can go back to school to change the focus of your work. You can team teach with others so you can learn about alternative strategies and styles. You can switch teaching assignments or schools. Or you can do it a more difficult way: You can stay in the same position but make significant changes in the ways you do it.

In spite of all the specific suggestions we have made and how hungry you are for even more detailed advice, there is a bigger picture to think about. Don't sweat the small stuff. Your main priority during your first year of teaching is to successfully complete it with your sanity, health, and enthusiasm intact, taking pride in what you have accomplished. Without that, you won't have a second year or a third.

The best teachers you ever had were able to convince you, on a primary level, that you had something important to offer others. That is your real job—to find the best that children have to offer and help them to discover this potential for themselves.

Resources
for Further
Reading

Arnold, H. (2001). *Succeeding in the secondary classroom: Strategies for middle and high school teachers.* Thousand Oaks, CA: Corwin.

Bevel, P. S., & Jordan, M. M. (2003). *Rethinking classroom management: Strategies for prevention, intervention, and problem solving.* Thousand Oaks, CA: Corwin.

Cattani, D. H. (2002). *A classroom of her own: How new teachers develop instructional, professional, and cultural competence.* Thousand Oaks, CA: Corwin.

Emmer, E. T., Everston, C. M., & Worsham, M. E. (2003). *Classroom management for secondary teachers.* Upper Saddle River, NJ: Pearson Education.

Guillaume, A. M. (2000). *Classroom teaching: A primer for new professionals.* Thousand Oaks, CA: Corwin.

Kottler, E., & Kottler, J. (2002). *Children with limited English: Teaching strategies for the regular classroom.* Thousand Oaks, CA: Corwin.

Kottler, J., & Kottler, E. (2000). *Counseling skills for teachers.* Thousand Oaks, CA: Corwin.

Kronowitz, E. L. (1999). *Your first year of teaching and beyond.* Menlo Park, CA: Longman.

Oosterhof, A. (2003). *Developing and using classroom assessments.* Upper Saddle River, NJ: Pearson Education.

Maing, M. L., & Bucher, K. T. (2003). *Classroom management: Models, applications, and cases.* Upper Saddle River, NJ: Pearson Education.

Marzano, R. (2003). *What works in schools: Translating research into action.* Alexandria, VA: Association for Supervision and Curriculum Development.

Marzano, R., Pickering, D. J., & Pollack, J. E. (2001). *Classroom instruction that works: Research-based strategies for increasing student achievement.* Alexandria, VA: Association for Supervision and Curriculum Development.

Nielson, L. B. (2002). *Brief Reference of student disabilities . . . with strategies for the classroom.* Thousand Oaks, CA: Corwin.

Pelletier, C. M. (2000). *Strategies for successful student teaching: A comprehensive guide.* Needham Heights: MA: Allyn & Bacon.

Price, K. M., & Nelson, K. L. (2003). *Daily planning for today's classroom: A guide for writing lesson & activity plans.* Belmont, CA: Wadsworth/Thomson Learning.

Spinelli, C. G. (2002). *Classroom assessment for students with special needs in inclusive settings.* Upper Saddle River, NJ: Pearson Education.

Wiggins, G., & McTighe, J. (1998). *Understanding by design.* Alexandria, VA: Association for Supervision and Curriculum Development.

Index